BATTLE
OF
TREVILIAN STATION

THE CIVIL WAR'S GREATEST AND BLOODIEST ALL CAVALRY BATTLE

With Eyewitness Memoirs

WALBROOK DAVIS SWANK
Colonel, USAF Ret.

BATTLE OF TREVILIAN STATION
The Civil War's Greatest and Bloodiest All Cavalry Battle

With Eyewitness Memoirs

This Burd Street Press publication
was printed by
Beidel Printing House, Inc.
63 West Burd Street
Shippensburg, PA 17257 USA

For a complete list of available publications
please write
Burd Street Press
Division of White Mane Publishing Company, Inc.
P.O. Box 152
Shippensburg, PA 17257 USA

In respect for the scholarship contained herein, the acid-free paper used in this book meets the guidelines for permanence and durability of the Committee on Production Guidelines for Book Longevity of the Council on Library Resources.

Library of Congress Cataloging-in-Publication Data

Swank, Walbrook D. (Walbrook Davis)
      Battle of Trevilian station : the Civil War's greatest and
bloodiest all cavalry battle, with eyewitness memoirs / Walbrook
Davis Swank.
         p.   cm.
      Includes bibliographical references (p.) and index.
      ISBN 0-942597-68-0 : $14.99
      1. Trevilian Station, Battle of, Va., 1864.   I. Title.
E476.6.S93   1994
973.7'37--dc20   94-14452
                                                CIP

Cover art, "The Gray Wall" by Don Troiani, photo courtesy Historical Art Prints, Ltd., Southbury, Connecticut.

PRINTED IN THE UNITED STATES OF AMERICA

Also By The Author

Clash of Sabres — Blue and Gray

The War and Louisa County, 1861-1865

Train Running for the Confederacy, 1861-1865
An Eyewitness Memoir

Confederate War Stories, 1861-1865

Eyewitness to War, 1861-1865

Courier for Lee and Jackson

And
The Award Winning

Confederate Letters & Diaries, 1861-1865

DEDICATION

In Memory of the
Courage, Patriotism and Devotion of the
Soldiers of the Confederate States of America.

"A people who have not the pride to record their history, will not long have the virtue to make history that is worth recording; and no people who are indifferent to their past, need hope to make their future great."

Author Unknown

ILLUSTRATIONS

ILLUSTRATIONS *continued*

MAPS

CONTENTS

CONTENTS *continued*

Artifacts from the Field of Battle

ABOUT THE AUTHOR

During his distinguished career in the United States Air Force the author received numerous awards for meritorious service and at one time was a member of a Task Force in the Office of the Personnel Advisor to the President, The White House. Colonel Swank is a native of Harrisonburg, Virginia. His grandfather, Thomas S. Davis of Richmond, Virginia, was a member of the Tenth Virginia Cavalry and a relative of President Jefferson Davis. He has written or edited seven previous books about the North-South conflict, including his Award Winning *Confederate Letters and Diaries, 1861-1865*.

He has a Master's degree in American Military History and holds membership in the Bonnie Blue Society which is based on his scholarly research and published literature. He is the recipient of the United Daughters of the Confederacy's Jefferson Davis Medal for his outstanding contributions to the preservation and promotion of our Southern history and heritage.

He is a member of the Society of Civil War Historians, the Military Order of the Stars and Bars, Sons of the American Revolution, the Ohio State University Alumni Association and four Virginia historical societies.

ACKNOWLEDGMENTS

I am indebted, and express my appreciation, to these contributors, and others, who helped make this work possible.

William G. Ryckman, Lecturer in Business Administration (Retired), Graduate School of Business Administration, University of Virginia, Charlottesville, Virginia, for permission to use material from his work *Clash of Cavalry at Trevilians.*

Mrs. M.H. Harris of West Point, Virginia, for the use of information from her husband's book *A History of Louisa County, Virginia.*

King McLaurin of St. Petersburg, Florida, for Private Edward L. Well's *Sketch of the Charleston Light Dragoons*, Fourth South Carolina Cavalry, and letter of his ancestor, First Lieutenant Allen Edens of the same regiment.

Robert B. Wilkinson, Jr., of St. Matthews, South Carolina, for information regarding his ancestor Private Francis M. Moorer of the Fifth South Carolina Cavalry, who was mortally wounded at the Battle of Trevilian Station, Virginia, and the story of the war by Private Augustus Law of the Sixth South Carolina Cavalry.

Colonel Murray F. Rose, USMC Ret., of Paeonian Springs, Virginia, for information pertaining to Private Isaac S. Curtis of the Ninth Virginia Cavalry.

John Nicholas Davis of Woodstock, Virginia, a cousin of the writer, for John Gill's *Reminiscences of Four Years As A Private Soldier.*

William H. Kiblinger of Mineral, Virginia, for information about the Yankee sabre found on the battlefield at Trevilian Station, Virginia, by his uncle, Hiram H. Kiblinger of Louisa, Virginia.

Louise D. Tucker of Greenville, South Carolina, for data regarding her ancestor, Private David Carter Ridgeway of the Sixth South Carolina Cavalry.

Elton Strong of Mineral, Virginia, for the display of his battlefield artifacts and those of Alvin Watson of Gordonsville, Virginia.

Christine Denton of Keswick, Virginia, for the reminiscences of Sergeant B.J. Haden, her ancestor.

The University of North Carolina at Chapel Hill, Chapel Hill, North Carolina.

The Department of Archives and History, Atlanta, Georgia.

The Jones Memorial Library, Lynchburg, Virginia.

FOREWORD

Situated on the gently rolling terrain of the Piedmont Region of Central Virginia, and in the center of the triangle formed by Charlottesville, Fredericksburg and Richmond, amidst the quiet countryside of Louisa County, is the little village of Trevilians. Through this village runs the same railroad that was part of the vital Virginia Central Railroad during the war years of 1861-1865. The Louisa County Court House is just several miles east of the railroad station in the village. In this area the greatest and bloodiest all cavalry battle of the War Between the States was fought. From the railroad station, post office and village market, one can see the state's Historical Marker across the road on US 33/SR 22 which is shown below:

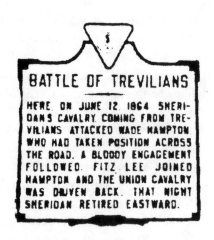

BATTLE OF TREVILIANS

HERE ON JUNE 12 1864 SHERI-
DANS CAVALRY COMING FROM TRE-
VILIANS ATTACKED WADE HAMPTON
WHO HAD TAKEN POSITION ACROSS
THE ROAD. A BLOODY ENGAGEMENT
FOLLOWED. FITZ LEE JOINED
HAMPTON AND THE UNION CAVALRY
WAS DRIVEN BACK. THAT NIGHT
SHERIDAN RETIRED EASTWARD.

INTRODUCTION

This narrative is the most detailed and complete account of the Battle of Trevilian Station, the greatest and bloodiest all cavalry battle of the War Between the States. An added, unusual, and prominent feature is the inclusion of many eyewitness memoirs of exciting events as seen by those who participated in this intense struggle between approximately 5,000 gray clad Confederate cavalrymen and about 8,000 blue coated Union troopers who fought mostly dismounted.

Some historians may consider the Battle of Brandy Station the greatest cavalry engagement of the war because over 20,000 Blue and Gray troops were involved; however, Union General Alfred Pleasanton's force included eight regiments of infantry and a battery of artillery—3,000 men under Generals Adelbert Ames and Daniel Russell. There were no separate infantry or artillery units involved in the action at Trevilian Station.

Major General Wade Hampton's magnificent leadership prevented Union Major General Philip Sheridan and his numerically superior and better equipped troops from severely damaging the vital Virginia Central Railroad that carried vital provisions and war material from the Shenandoah Valley to General Robert E. Lee's hard pressed army located around Richmond. Additionally, and more importantly, it denied Sheridan his objective of joining Major General David Hunter in Charlottesville or Lexington where a united force could strike out down the James River towards Richmond and Petersburg and attack General Lee's army from the west.

In a report to the Union Army's Chief of Staff on June 16th Sheridan gave his reasons for not advancing farther towards Charlottesville and concludes by saying, "I regret my inability to carry out your instructions".

In reviewing the many eyewitness accounts of the Blue and Gray combatants of 1861-1865, there are none more prominent or impressive than those about the Battle of Trevilian Station that are recorded here.

The first hand accounts of battle actions, hardships and experiences are vividly brought out by these men who were locked in heated combat on two hot days in June of 1864 in the greatest and bloodiest all cavalry battle of the war. When the blazing guns ceased firing on the night of the 12th, the conflict between the Blue and the Gray had left over 2,000 casualties.

Chapter I

THE VIRGINIA CENTRAL RAILROAD AND TREVILIAN STATION

Before we discuss the Battle of Trevilian Station let us review the nature and operation of the strategically and logistically important Virginia Central Railroad which was the main target of Union General Philip Sheridan's attack.

The tracks of the Virginia Central Railroad ran from Richmond to Hanover Junction, then west through Louisa, Gordonsville and Charlottesville to Staunton. From there the rails turned south to the end of the line at Jackson's River. At Gordonsville and Charlottesville the Virginia Central intersected the Orange and Alexandria Railroad that ran to Lynchburg and from that point other lines led to Chattanooga and Atlanta.

Edward Fontaine, president of the road, was a northerner by birth, but he performed notable and loyal services to his adopted country during the war. His salary was $4,500 a year, and in 1864 a barrel of oil, forty-two and a half gallons, cost $4,250 in the depreciated Confederate currency. In 1862 the entire cost to the railroad for oil, tallow, lard and grease consumed was only $3,645.48. If Fontaine was worth only a barrel of oil to the road, he was a more valuable commodity than J.H. Whitlock, the station agent at Trevilians whose $450 salary in 1861 had been increased to $2,100 in 1864.

The railroad owned several hundred slaves, thirty-five of which had been purchased in 1863 for $83,484, and more were desperately needed to cut wood for the engines and ties for the roadbed if the railroad was to continue to be a major supply artery to Richmond and General Lee's army.

Business at Whitlock's station was poor in 1864. In May only nineteen passengers had arrived at Trevilians, and he had sold only forty-five tickets in the whole month. Back in 1860 the average had been a hundred passengers a month, arrivals and departures, too. Freight tonnage was only a quarter of what it had been four years earlier.

Fontaine was proud of the men who ran the railroad under such trying conditions and perhaps his favorite was Superintendent H.D. Whitcomb who had issued pungent instructions to his crews in Charlottesville in the spring of 1862 when General Jackson's army was transported from the Valley to aid in the defense of Richmond. "In consideration of the enormous task of moving such an army with so limited power," he had said, "I would be glad to have one sober man on each crew and think it best not to put all the whiskey men together."

Maintenance was becoming a more serious problem every month to Fontaine. An engine drawing the standard load of fifteen freight cars burned a cord of wood every fifty or sixty miles, and cordwood as well as ties were in short supply. Raiding Union cavalry had learned that burning supplies of wood and ties caused almost as much disruption as tearing up track. Rails themselves were a continuing problem. Made of malleable iron, they wore out quickly, and when the enemy tore them up, heated them over a fire of ties and bent them around a tree, the rails, weighing seventy pounds a yard, had to be reprocessed in the rolling mill before reuse. It was customary to lay ties on bare gound, using no ballast, and grading was done only when absolutely necessary.

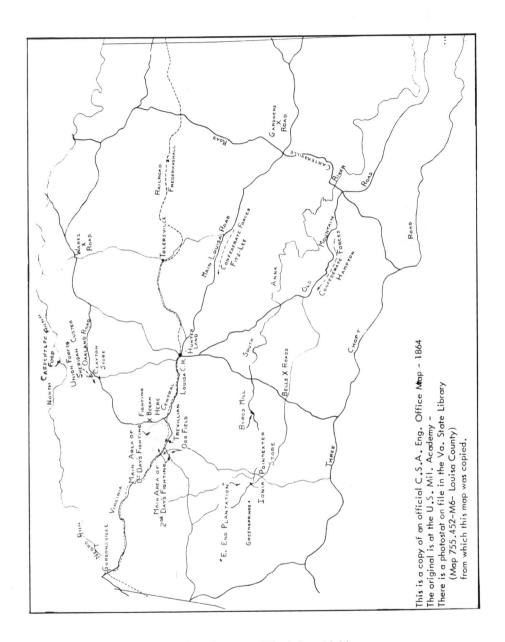

This is a copy of an official C.S.A. Eng. Office Map - 1864
The original is at the U.S. Mil. Academy -
There is a photostat on file in the Va. State Library
(Map 755.452-M6- Louisa County)
from which this map was copied.

Louisa County, Virginia, 1864

Chapter II

BATTLE OF TREVILIAN STATION

Over the years, historians, writers and students of the War Between the States have failed to give the Battle of Trevilians the attention, publicity or recognition that this military engagement deserves. Accordingly, public awareness of its importance is not widely known. Little has been published about the battle, which was a cavalry fight, but most of it was fought by dismounted troopers with firepower, as usual, favoring the bluecoats because of their primary use of Spencer repeating rifles.

Lieutenant General Ulysses S. Grant, President Abraham Lincoln's Commander of the Federal Army, on the 26th of May, 1864, sent Major General David Hunter up the Shenandoah Valley with 18,000 men to pillage, burn, and wreak destruction in the Valley which was General Robert E. Lee's main source of food and supplies for his army. These military necessities were shipped over the Virginia Central Railroad through Charlottesville, Gordonsville, and Louisa to Richmond and Petersburg battle areas. Hunter's primary objective was to capture Lexington and Lynchburg where he expected to cut the James River Canal and the Southside Railroad, which led to Richmond, and go on to Charlottesville and make contact with Major General Philip Sheridan.

The latter, on the 6th of June, at New Castle Ferry, issued his troops three days' rations and two days' grain for the horses. The rations consisted of thirty-six biscuits (hardtack), nine tablespoons each of coffee and sugar. In addition, forty rounds of ammunition were given to each man. An ammunition reserve of sixty rounds per man was carried in the wagon train which also included a medical wagon and eight ambulances. Each division and brigade headquarters was alloted one wagon and eight canvas covered boats, enough for a short pontoon bridge.

On June 7th, Sheridan, Commander, Cavalry Corps, Army of the Potomac, with about 8,000 horsemen, left Grant's army at New Castle, crossed the North Anna River at Carpenter's Ford and into Louisa County on June 10th. The long column, including four batteries of horse artillery and a long train of about 125 wagons stretched four miles along the road. The weather was dry and hot. There had been no sustained rain for over two weeks and the roads were thick with dust which rose in heavy clouds kicked up by the horses and wagons. Forage in the devastated area was almost nil. Two days later 250 weakened horses were lost and saddles and equipment were carried in wagons and the men continued the march on foot.

They bivouacked at Clayton's Store several miles north of Trevilian Station. As part of Grant's plan, Sheridan was to tear up the Virginia Central Railroad somewhere between Gordonsville and Louisa and cut off Lee's supply line to the Valley and join Hunter in the vicinity of Charlottesville.

Meanwhile, on June 8th, Major General Wade Hampton, Commander, Cavalry Corps of the Army of Northern Virginia, encamped at Atlee, was advised by Lee of Sheridan's movement and ordered him to take his division and that of Major General Fitz Lee, numbering about 5,000 cavalrymen, follow Sheridan and interpose his command between him and the railroad.

Hampton led his troopers up the Brook Turnpike, turned off on the Telegraph Road to Hanover Junction, and going westward, arrived at Hewletts at sunset. Here the gray clad horsemen dismounted to feed the horses and then marched on to Beverdam Station where they camped that night. At daylight the column moved on and passed through Frederick's Hall and reached Louisa Court House in late afternoon on the 10th.

As darkness closed in, Hampton and Brigadier General Thomas L. Rosser camped in the Green Springs area on the Gordonsville road about three miles west of Trevilians. Brigadier General M.C. Butler's brigade bivouacked around Trevilian Station with Colonel G.J. Wright's command to the east and Major General Fitz Lee's Division camped on the east side of Louisa Court House.

A short distance to the east of the Station, the highway made a loop on the north side of the tracks. The road south from Clayton's Store met the main road at the center of the loop and nearby was the Tavern, a frame building with two stories and an attic. The inn was not of the best quality, accommodations or cuisine, but was the only resting place between Louisa Court House and Gordonsville. Not far from the Tavern was the home of the Netherlands, one of the prominent families in the vicinity.

On Friday night, June 10th, in a horse lot in an oak grove in front of the Netherlands' home Hampton spent the night sleeping fully dressed on a

Major Williston, then a lieutenant, was in command of Horse Battery D, Second U.S. Artillery.

carpenter's bench. It was here that Generals Thomas Rosser and Matthew Butler found him after sunrise on Saturday morning. They asked what were his intentions; "I propose to fight," came his reply.

On Saturday morning, the 11th, Captain Milligan of the Fourth South Carolina Cavalry of Brigadier General Matthew C. Butler's South Carolina Brigade met a heavy force of Union troopers supported by Williston's battery of artillery along the road and in the dense woods south of Clayton's Store and north of Trevilian Station. Butler dismounted his men and disposed them in the woods, sending their horses to the rear.

Union General Alfred Torbert had lost contact with his youthful, long-curly-haired General George Custer but pressed forward. When the Fourth and Ninth New York Cavalry worked alongside of the road, they came to a wide open area in the forest. On a ridge and surrounded by an orchard stood the Poindexter house. This was the center of the Confederate line which now was within three miles of the station. Torbert was at the front and ordered the two New York regiments to charge the house and orchard. Lieutenant Colonel William Sackett of the Ninth New York gave the order "Forward", and led his nearly three hundred blue horsemen towards the house. Within minutes a bullet struck his abdomen and he fell, mortally wounded. Forty others of his command were hit and left the field as the regiment continued its charge and joined the Fourth New York in capturing the objective, taking a number of prisoners in the process. Lieutenant Colonel George S. Nichols succeeded in command.

7

Trevilian Station today. It is used as the Post Office. At the time of the war it was located across the railroad tracks to the right of this picture.

The wounded officer, along with several other severely wounded men, was moved to the home of Mrs. Bibb who lived in a log hut a short distance up the road toward Clayton's Store. The officer was laid on the only bed in the house and was left behind when Sheridan retreated on the night of the 12th. He died of his wound on the evening of the 14th and was buried near Mrs. Bibb's home the following day.

Lieutenant Colonel William Sackett, Ninth New York Cavalry

8

Later, as Butler was being slowly forced back toward the railroad, a number of his men took shelter in the Tavern. Its sturdy timbers provided good protection for the troops firing from the windows of both floors and the attic. The dismounted Federals attacked from three sides. During a brief lull in the fighting, the door of the Tavern was pushed open and a woman ran out on the road. It was Mrs. Lucy Hughson, carrying her baby in her arms. A sharp command rang out, the Union carbines were silenced and the Confederates held their fire.

Captain H.C. Orme, a Federal officer from Phoenix, Arizona, saw Mrs. Hughson's dilemma. He galloped forward, lifting the baby from her arms and escorted both mother and baby to safety. Not until the little group had disappeared from the sight of the blue and gray troopers did the firing resume.

Meantime, Union General George Custer, with his Michigan regiments, came out of the woods along a farm road about two and a half miles to the east toward Louisa, moved westward and captured Thomson's artillery battery, the horses and Hampton's wagon train which was parked in a field across the road from the station. Major R.P. Chew, Commander of Hampton's battalion of artillery, however, deployed a South Carolina regiment to hold

Netherland Tavern—The old tavern at Trevilians which was riddled by shot and shell during the battle. Here, Mrs. Lucy Hughson carried baby in arms across field at Trevilians in 1864 during bitter engagement.

9

back Custer's men until he could get another battery into position. Shortly, from the Louisa Court House area Fitz Lee's men pressed the First Michigan, guarding Custer's rear, and Thomas Rosser with his Laurel Brigade arrived and recaptured the horses and wagons in addition to that of Custer's, including his personal baggage wagon.

The following is a report submitted by General Rosser on June 30th, 1864, which gives his account of the battle in which he suffered a painful leg wound. "After I had dismounted my brigade about two miles west of Trevilian Station and was waiting to hear from scouts which I had sent out around the right flank of the enemy to ascertain if he were moving toward Gordonsville, a trooper from Young's brigade came galloping up from the rear with a saber cut across his face, and reported that the enemy had gotten in the rear of Young's and Butler's brigades, which were fighting on foot, and had captured the division wagon train and the horses of the dismounted men of these two brigades. I ordered a company to mount and go back and see if this report were true, but before it started off, several more men from the same command came running at full speed, yelling 'Yankees! Yankees!' I then mounted the brigade at once and riding at the head of it went back at a brisk trot in the direction whence these men had come.

Scrub oaks, almost a 'chaparral,' covered the ground on each side of the narrow road, and as the road was very crooked, I could not see a stone's throw ahead of men, and, expecting to find the enemy at or near the station, I was as much surprised as he appeared to be, when, turning a sharp curve in the road, I came immediately on him. It was Custer's brigade, which had passed around Butler's right between him and Fitzhugh Lee, had gotten in the rear of the former and captured the wagon train and the horses of the two brigades then fighting on foot. Not expecting trouble from the direction from which I came, Custer had not taken the precaution of putting pickets on that road, and thinking when he saw the head of my column that it was only a scouting party, he wheeled so as to meet the charge which I sounded on the sight of him; but I was too quick and too strong for him, and as I went crashing into him, breaking up and scattering his squadrons, he made a gallant and manly effort to resist me. Sitting on his horse in the midst of his advanced platoons, and near enough to be easily recognized by me, he encouraged and inspired his men by appeal as well as by example. His color-sergeant was shot down at his side, by Major Holmes Conrad, of my staff, when Custer grabbed the staff to save his flag, but the death-grip of the sergeant would not release it, so, with a quick jerk, Custer tore the flag from its staff and in triumph carried it off. Closely pursuing, I recaptured our men, horses and wagons, as well as many prisoners from the enemy, and drove Custer back, with heavy loss, into Sheridan's lines.''

Rosser's Cavalry Charge

The above picture shows General Wade Hampton leading ''The Cadet Charge'' at the Louisa County, Virginia, Court House which was the prelude to the Battle of Trevilian Station.

Courtesy of the Archives Museum, The Citadel, Charleston, South Carolina

In 1862 thirty-six cadets of the Citadel College in South Carolina, with some cadets from the Arsenal, became a part of the Sixth South Carolina Cavalry. This troop was with General Wade Hampton's cavalry at Louisa Court House on June 11, 1864 as the Battle of Trevilians began.

Lieutenant Alfred Aldrich of the Company gave this account of the skirmish:

> During the fight, Hart's Battery was charged by a Column of the Enemy Cavalry when our line was in confusion passing thru a railroad excavation. General Hampton dashed up to the right of the Sixth Cavalry to get a force to follow him in a charge to save the Battery, and although the confusion was great at this part of the line as elsewhere, thanks to the Citadel training, Lieutenant Nettles and Aldrich got their company aligned in a few seconds and General Hampton charged in line of battle with the Cadet Company staying the enemy's onset.

This colorful charge of the Cadet Company with General Wade Hampton is the subject of a mural placed in the new library at the Citadel. General Wade Hampton and his horse, Butler, are easily recognized.

Hampton appointed one of Rosser's officers, Colonel Richard Dulany, Commanding the Seventh Virginia Cavalry, to command the Laurel Brigade in the absence of the injured Rosser.

A brisk fight went on all day with Hampton finally taking up a strong position several miles west of the railroad station while Fitz Lee was driven towards Louisa Court House.

During the night of the 11th, Lee moved his tired and worn out force by a circuitous route to reinforce Hampton who had entrenched behind earthworks on a ridge about two miles west of the railroad station in the Green Springs area across the Gordonsville and Charlottesville roads. Here his men found forage and good water but had only hardtack for subsistence.

Blue and Gray forces swayed back and forth all day with the advantage going to one side and then the other, but as the long day closed the Union troops had much the better of it. Sheridan held the area around the railroad at Trevilians and General Butler's statement that "This day's operations ended disastrously to our arms" confirmed the true situation.

On Sunday the 12th, Sheridan made seven unsuccessful attacks by dismounted troops on Hampton's line but was thrown back with heavy losses. A short distance in front of Hampton's line and about three hundred yards from the railroad stood a house surrounded by tall oaks. In it resided the Ogg family, a well-to-do farm family. The highway crossed the tracks at the east end of the embankment and a store owned by a man named Dennis

12

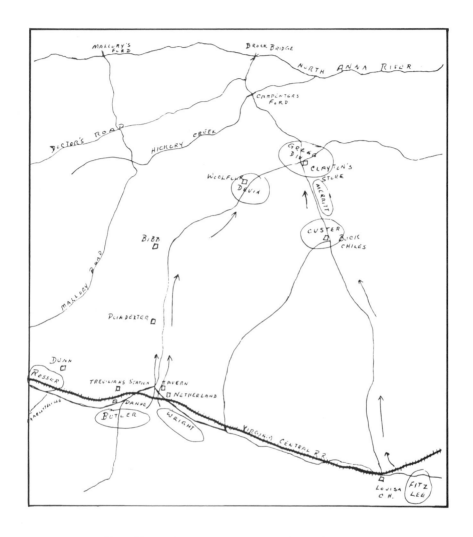

**Trevilians Area showing location of camps
on the night of June 10, 1864**

Arrows show Hampton's attack plans for June 11

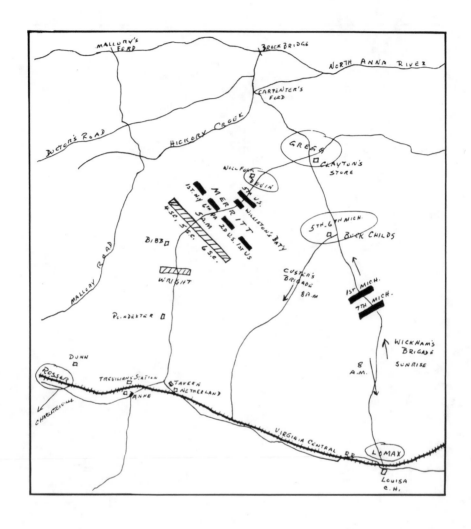

**Trevilians Battlefield
June 11, 1864**

Early Morning

14

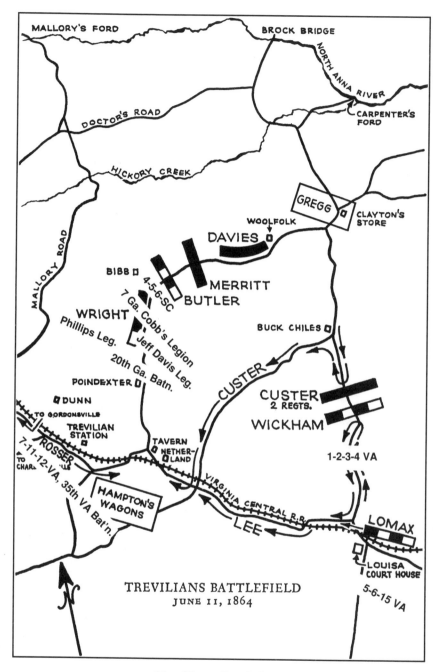

Trevilians Battlefield
June 11, 1864

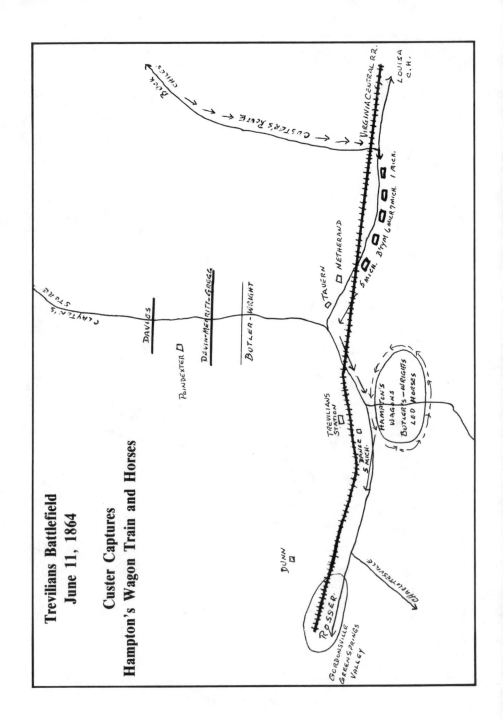

Trevilians Battlefield
June 11, 1864

Custer Captures
Hampton's Wagon Train and Horses

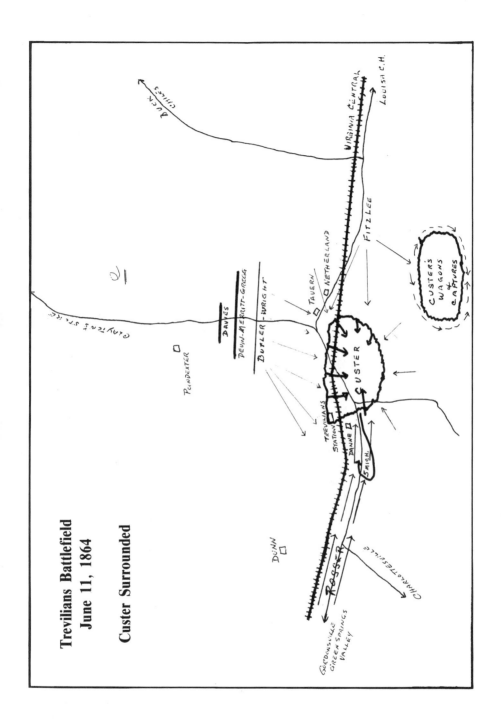

Trevilians Battlefield
June 11, 1864

Custer Surrounded

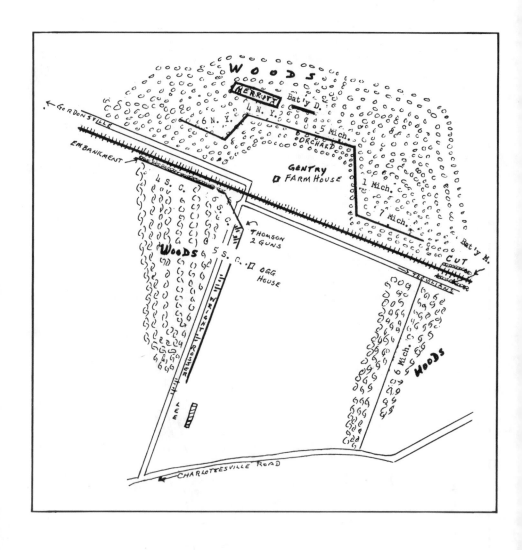

Trevilians Battlefield
June 12, 1864

Opening Positions

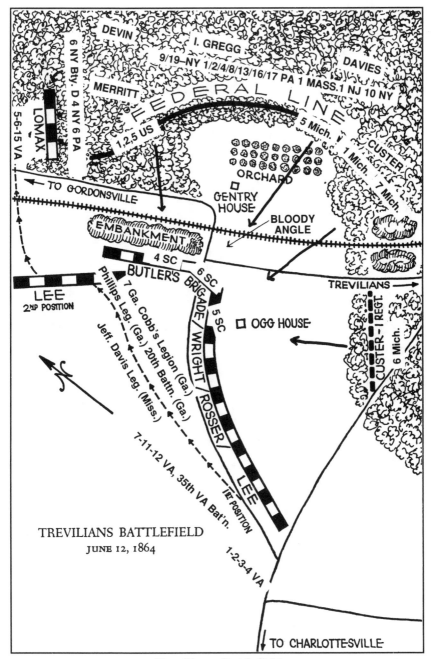

Trevilians Battlefield

June 12, 1864

Final Action

The old Danne Home. General Custer had his headquarters on the front porch during the battle in June, 1864.

was located near the crossing. It has been reported that the only civilian casualty of the battle occurred when a woman, trapped in the store between the lines, was killed by a bullet.

Across the tracks from the Ogg house as a large clearing. Here was located the Gentry house and behind it was an orchard that sheltered many Union troops on that hot Sabbath day.

Mr. and Mrs. Ogg, who had taken refuge in the basement, came upstairs along with a woman slave and her young son when Hampton's men arrived in the morning. The young boy had spent several very exciting hours watching the Confederates ready their position.

His delight turned to terror when Union Lieutenant A.C.M. Pennington's Battery M of the Second U.S. Artillery fired its first shell which exploded nearby, and he later remarked that he ran for five miles before stopping to take a breath. His mother spent the long day in a dirt cellar beneath the house, and when the fighting finally subsided at ten o'clock, she crawled out of her hiding place and rejoined the Oggs who had spent the time in the basement.

The above picture illustrates the cavalry's method of destroying railroads. The rails were placed across piles of ties. When the ties were fired the metal got hot and because of the weight they bent out of shape. Note the tangle of telegraph lines which were also torn up.

The main action centered around the railway cut and the Gentry house, but Custer's men in the woods to the east of Hampton's line, behind the Ogg house, kept up a steady fire so that the house could truly be said to be a no-man's-land. At one point, when a squad of South Carolinians were ordered to the Ogg house to do sharpshooting, five men were shot down before they reached the trees surrounding the place, and the survivors retreated.

All day, while the Federals made one charge after another at the angle in the Confederate line at the embankment, sharpshooters, concealed in the Danne house, had poured effective fire into the Confederate works. A gun was ordered up and, although standing unprotected in the meadow and a target for carbine and artillery fire, it succeeded in setting the house ablaze and drove out the occupants.

Fighting around the Ogg house had been intense and when darkness came the home was used as a hospital. The dining room table was covered with a blanket and made into an operating table amid the dim light of oil lamps as the surgeons went to work with their crude instruments and medicines trying to mend the torn and shattered bodies of casualties brought to them. Straw was placed on the floor to absorb some of the blood spilled when amputating arms and legs.

All day Sunday details of Federal troops scoured the countryside seeking wheeled vehicles. They brought back an amazing assortment of buggies, gigs, carriages and carts, drawn by an equally odd collection of aged horses and decrepit mules, leaving the county residents with scarcely any means of transportation. The conveyances were packed with wounded blue clad troopers as were Sheridan's eight ambulances, all ammunition wagons and many baggage wagons.

Ninety of the most severely wounded had to be left behind in three field hospitals, but in its retreat from Trevilians Sheridan's force was accompanied by 377 casualties and 370 prisoners, including 20 officers. His situation was critical. He was deep in enemy country and his ammunition reserves were almost exhausted. Conditions of both men and animals were poor and he had to feed 7,000 men as well as more than that number of horses. Moreover, hundreds of Negroes had attached themselves to his column and clung to it like leeches. From Sunday on they came in ever increasing numbers; men, women and children. Their worldly possessions were packed in pathetic little bundles which included little if any food. These people too, had to be fed, and their numbers soon reached 2,000.

*Lieutenant Alexander
C.M. Pennington,
Second U.S. Artillery, U.S.A.*

It was ten o'clock that night when the final fighting ended. Sheridan, believing that Confederate General John Breckinridge was at Charlottesville and had re-enforced Hampton during the night and in view of his heavy losses and shortage of ammunition, decided it was unwise to try to join Hunter. After destroying several miles of railroad track he withdrew his troops shortly after midnight, camping across the North Anna at Twyman's Store.

Because of the condition of Hampton's men and horses no move was made to pursue Sheridan until daylight at which time scouting parties were sent out to keep in touch with the retreating enemy.

On Monday morning Hampton sent Captain Zimmerman Davis, Commander of the Second Squadron of the Fifth South Carolina, to scour the battlefields, bury the dead, look after any wounded and gather up such abandoned arms as could be of service. Davis found that Sheridan had left behind him three hospitals with ninety Union soldiers and many Confederates. He also left a supply of medicines, liquor, hardtack, coffee and sugar. Assistant Surgeon Sickler of the Tenth New York and several attendants were caring for those left behind. Residents in the area treated all the wounded with tender care and all those who could be moved were brought to the railroad and taken to the Gordonsville hospital in construction cars which had no springs and were open to the weather. The wounded, clad in blue and gray, waited patiently for the cars and were ministered to by the women of the neighborhood who brought with them whatever meager supplies and bandages that were left to them.

The Ogg house

This picture shows how the Surgeon's operating room in the Ogg house probably looked when it was turned into a hospital. Amputated limbs were usually thrown in heaps outside the window.

Aside from field hospitals that had been set up, others were established at the railroad station, the Tavern and the Methodist Church and Old Court House in Louisa.

Hampton followed the retreating invaders day after day, and in the hundred miles of road between Trevilians and the White House on the Pamunkey River two thousand horses were found shot through the head.

The Confederates clung to Sheridan's right flank day after day. Scouting parties were in constant contact but no major clashes occurred until Sheridan was forced to fight at Jones Bridge on June 23rd and at St. Mary's Church the following day. It was not until July 2nd, after fifty-six consecutive days of marching and fighting, that Sheridan, after having rejoined Grant's army, was able to settle down and rest and refit his columns at Light-House Point.

When J.H. Whitlock, the station agent at Trevilians, reported for work on Monday morning following Sheridan's retreat he was distressed and discouraged when he reviewed the damage to his station. The depot was in ashes although the Danne house across the tracks still stood, scarred as it was with bullet and shell holes. The lovely flowers along the front of the house were broken and scattered on the ground. The watering station was demolished and blackened wheel carriages were all that remained of several good cars that had been standing nearby. Shortly, however, Whitlock was cheered as workers and materials began to arrive. It was discovered that three and a half miles of track had been torn up and ties burned. Ties were cut, new rails laid and eleven days later, on June 24th the road was again open for traffic.

Down the road, at Louisa Court House, was Oakland Cemetery, and for days after the battle its old iron gates stood open as grave after grave was dug and ninety-four nameless bodies of blue and gray clad soldiers were placed in graves. Neat rows of small and plain headstones marked the resting places of South Carolinians, Georgians and Virginians and those of young men from New York, Michigan or half a dozen other states north of the Mason and Dixon Line — Americans all. One day too, an imposing monument would identify the grave of Colonel J.L. McAllister of the Seventh Georgia and next to it would be a monument to a Captain Hines, of the same regiment, killed the same day. Not far away another name would have to be carved in a stone column erected by the Reverend John Towles to his two sons who had already given their all to the cause; J. Vivian, killed October 1, 1863 and James H., May 9, 1864. The new inscription would list twenty-year-old Robert C. Towles, Fourth Virginia Cavalry, wounded June 11, 1864, died June 16.

25

The two grave markers in the foreground are those of Colonel J.L. McAllister, left, and Captain Hines, right, who were killed at the Battle of Trevilians while fighting with the Seventh Georgia Cavalry. They are among nearly one hundred soldiers — both Union and Confederate — who are buried in Oakland Cemetery at Louisa, Virginia.

Louisa attorney John Gilmer is the only known local resident who has a relative from another Southern state that took part in the battle. Gilmer's great-grandfather was John Monroe of Company H of the same regiment as the officers named above. He was wounded in the right arm in the fight and his horse was killed. He returned to his home, near Savannah, in Liberty County, Georgia. The attorney has a sabre that was found, with other items, just after the battle and taken to the Danne house. He surmises that the weapon may have belonged to his ancestor.

Although the Battle of Brandy Station is recognized as the greatest cavalry battle of the war with over 20,000 Union and Confederate troops engaged, the number of casualties were less than those in the Battle of Trevilians. At Brandy General J.E.B. Stuart had 523 casualties while Union General Pleasanton lost 936.

In the battles on June 11th and 12th Sheridan lost 93 men and nine officers; 438 men and thirty-two officers were wounded and 427 men and eight officers were captured or missing — for a total of 1,007 casualties.

At a special ceremony on Saturday, June 12, 1982, at 10:30 a.m., the Mineral Chapter, United Daughters of the Confederacy, donated and dedicated a handsome monument at Oakland Cemetery in Louisa, Virginia, in memory of nearly one hundred men, Union and Confederate — Americans all — who were killed at the Battle of Trevilians, June 11-12, 1864.

Members of the Mineral Chapter, United Daughters of the Confederacy. Left to right are Mrs. W.A. Weldey, Past Chapter President, Mrs. Herschal Shank, a Real Daughter, Mrs. Walbrook D. Swank, Past Chapter President, Mrs. Edmund Meredith, Past Chapter President and Past President Virginia Division, United Daughters of the Confederacy.

Hampton's losses are difficult to determine. The official report of his operations June 8-24, 1864 states that in his Division alone he lost 59 killed, 258 wounded and 295 missing in the two days at Trevilians. There is no record of Fitz Lee's losses. It is estimated that his were about 75% of Hampton's and if the assumption is correct we must add 459 casualties to Hampton's total of 612, making a total of 1,071, which is 64 greater than Sheridan's loss. This would represent a loss of over 20% of the Confederate strength compared to 12% of the Union.

Let us now assess the results accomplished by Hampton and Sheridan in the clash of arms along the Virginia Central Railroad in the countryside of Central Virginia on those two hot days in June of 1864.

Sheridan's plan was to (1) join Hunter at Charlottesville, destroy the Rivanna bridge there, (2) tear up the railroad from that point to Gordonsville, and (3) keep the Confederate Cavalry fully occupied while the Army of the Potomac delicately maneuvered east and south of Richmond in an attempt to take Petersburg and invest Richmond from the south. Sheridan did not meet Hunter, was not closer than thirty miles from Charlottesville and did only minor damage to the railroad. He was successful, however, in keeping General Robert E. Lee's two divisions of cavalry fully occupied, making it possible for Grant to move his base and army undetected and unimpeded.

Hampton, for his part, handled a difficult situation superbly. He was magnificently supported by General Butler of South Carolina who held Hampton's Division together on both days of the fighting and the green troopers of his three regiments exhibited the staunchness of the veterans of the Stonewall Brigade or Hood's Texans. General Tom Rosser likewise distinguished himself by the charge of his Laurel Brigade and may well have saved Butler, while Fitz Lee's movements lacked his normal vigorous pursuit of the enemy. Colonel Wright, commanding Young's Brigade, Wickham and Lomax discharged their duties admirably.

Sheridan paid only general tribute to his division and brigade commanders. General Torbert cited General Merritt and Colonel Devin for bravery and coolness in action on June 11 and Lieutenants Williston, Pennington and Heaton for their handling of the guns on both days of the battle. He credited Custer with saving his command under trying circumstances. General Gregg had little to report on either General Davies or Colonel J.I. Gregg.

Sheridan might have had a major tactical victory had he taken advantage of the opportunity to destroy first Fitz Lee and then Butler after they had been driven in opposite directions. With his concentrated and numerically superior force over Lee's division of four to one and three to one over Hampton, he made no attempt to exploit the advantage on either once the pressure was relaxed. Further, he made no attempt to follow the movements of the Confederates on the night of the 11th or the morning of the 12th.

In a report to Grant's Chief of Staff on June 16th he gives his reasons for not advancing further towards Charlottesville and concludes by saying, "I regret my inability to carry out your instructions."

The organization of the Confederate and Union Forces and the return of Casualties of Sheridan's Expedition is shown on the following pages.

CAVALRY CORPS

HAMPTON'S DIVISION

Maj. Gen. Wade Hampton

Young's Brigade

Col. G.J. Wright

7th Georgia, Col. William P. White
Cobb's (Georgia) Legion, Col. G.J. Wright
Phillips (Georgia) Legion, Lt. Col. Wm. W. Rich
20th Georgia Battalion, Lieut. Col. John
    M. Millen
Jeff. Davis (Mississippi) Legion, Col. J.F. Waring

Rosser's Brigade

Brig. Gen. Thomas L. Rosser

7th Virginia, Col. Richard H. Dulany
11th Virginia, Col. O.R. Funsten
12th Virginia, Lieut. Col. Thomas B.
    Massie
35th Virginia Battalion, Col. Elijah V.
    White

Butler's Brigade

Brig. Gen. Matthew C. Butler

4th South Carolina, Col. B. Huger Rutledge
5th South Carolina, Jam. John H. Morgan
6th South Carolina, Col. Hugh K. Aiken

FITZHUGH LEE'S DIVISION

Maj. Gen. Fitzhugh Lee

Lomax's Brigade

Brig. Gen. Lunsford L. Lomax

5th Virginia, Col. Henry C. Pate
6th Virginia, Col. John S. Green
15th Virginia, Col. Charles R. Collins

Wickham's Brigade

Brig. Gen. Williams C. Wickham

1st Virginia, Lt. Col. Wm. A. Morgan
2nd Virginia, Col. Thomas T. Munford
3rd Virginia, Col. Thomas H. Owen
4th Virginia, Col. Wm. B. Wooldridge

HORSE ARTILLERY

Maj. R. Preston Chew
Maj. James Breathed

Hart's South Carolina Battery
Johnston's Virginia Battery
Thomson's Virginia Battery

29

CAVALRY CORPS

Maj. Gen. Philip H. Sheridan

ESCORT

6th United States, Capt. Ira W. Cladin

FIRST DIVISION

Brig. Gen. Alfred T.A. Torbert

First Brigade	*Second Brigade*
Brig. Gen. George A. Custer	Col. Thomas C. Devin.
1st Michigan, Lieut. Col. Peter Stagg.	4th New York, Lieut. Col. William R. Parnell
5th Michigan, Col. Russell A. Alger	6th New York, Lieut. Col. William H. Crocker
6th Michigan, Maj. James H. Kidd	9th New York, Lieut. Col. George S. Nichols
7th Michigan, Maj. Alexander Walker	17th Pennsylvania, Lieut. Col. James Q. Anderson

Reserve Brigade

Brig. Gen. Wesley Merritt

19th New York (1st Dragoons), Col. Alfred Gibbs
6th Pennsylvania, Maj. William P.C. Treichel
1st United States, Capt. Nelson B. Sweitzer
2nd United States, Capt. Theophilus F. Rodenbough
5th United States, Capt. Abraham K. Arnold

SECOND DIVISION

Brig. Gen. David McM. Gregg

First Brigade	*Second Brigade*
Brig. Gen. Henry E. Davies, Jr.	Col. J. Irving Gregg
1st Massachusetts, Lieut. Col. Samuel E. Chamberlain	2nd Pennsylvania, Lieut. Col. Joseph P. Brintoh
1st New Jersey, Lieut. Col. John W. Kester	4th Pennsylvania, Lieut. Col. George H. Coyode
10th New York, Maj. M. Henry Avery	8th Pennsylvania, Col. Pernock Huey
1st Pennsylvania, Col. John P. Taylor	13th Pennsylvania, Maj. Michael Kerwin
	16th Pennsylvania, Lieut. Col. John K. Robison

HORSE ARTILLERY

1st United State Battery H and I, Lieut. Edward Heaton
2nd United State Battery D, Lieut. Edward B. Williston
2nd United States Battery M, Lieut. Alexander C.M. Pennington, Jr.

THE TREVILLIANS RAID, JUNE 7-24, 1864

Command.	Killed.		Wounded.		Captured or missing.		Aggregate.
	Officers.	Men.	Officers.	Men.	Officers.	Men.	
CAVALRY CORPS.							
Maj. Gen. PHILIP H. SHERIDAN.							
Trevilians Station and Newark (or Mallory's Cross-Roads), June 11-12, 1864.							
Headquarters Escort							
6th U. S. Cavalry	.....	.....	.....	3	.....	1	
FIRST DIVISION.							
Brig. Gen. ALFRED T. A. TORBERT							
First Brigade.							
Brig. Gen. GEORGE A. CUSTER.							
Staff	.....	.....	.....	.....	1	.....	1
1st Michigan	2	10	3	20	2	62	99
5th Michigan	.....	4	4	7	1	135	151
6th Michigan	.....	7	1	21	1	59	89
7th Michigan	.....	2	1	25	.....	48	76
Total First Brigade	2	23	9	73	5	304	416
Second Brigade.							
Col. THOMAS C. DEVIN.							
4th New York	1	5	5	27	.....	6	44
6th New York	.....	2	1	10	.....	27	40
9th New York	.....	4	3	38	.....	5	50
17th Pennsylvania	.....	5	.....	19	.....	2	26
Total Second Brigade	1	16	9	94	.....	40	160
Reserve Brigade.							
Brig. Gen. WESLEY MERRITT.							
19th New York (1st Dragoons)	.....	16	4	57	1	7	85
6th Pennsylvania	.....	6	1	55	.....	5	67
1st United States	2	6	1	31	.....	5	45
2d United States	1	7	2	36	1	4	51
5th United States	1	2	.....	6	.....	4	13
Total Reserve Brigade	4	37	8	185	2	25	261
Total First Division	7	76	26	352	7	369	837
SECOND DIVISION.							
Brig. Gen. DAVID McM. GREGG.							
First Brigade.							
Brig. Gen. HENRY E. DAVIES, Jr.							
1st Massachusetts	.....	.....	.....	.....	.....	2	2
1st New Jersey	.....	1	.....	2	.....	3	6
10th New York	1	3	1	15	.....	.....	20
1st Pennsylvania	.....	.....	.....	.....	.....	1	1
Total First Brigade	1	4	1	17	.....	6	29
Second Brigade.							
Col. J. IRVIN GREGG.							
2d Pennsylvania	1	.....	.....	5	.....	1	7
4th Pennsylvania	.....	2	3	23	1	2	31
8th Pennsylvania	.....	5	.....	16	.....	5	26
13th Pennsylvania	.....	1	.....	2	.....	6	9
16th Pennsylvania	.....	2	1	13	.....	.....	16
Total Second Brigade	1	10	4	59	1	14	89
Total Second Division	2	14	5	76	1	20	118

31

THE TREVILLIANS RAID, JUNE 7-24, 1864—Continued.

Command.	Killed.		Wounded.		Captured or missing.		Aggregate.
	Officers.	Men.	Officers.	Men.	Officers.	Men.	
HORSE ARTILLERY BRIGADE.							
Capt. JAMES M. ROBERTSON.							
1st United States, Batteries H and I		1	1				2
2d United States, Battery D				2			2
2d United States, Battery M		2		5		37	44
Total Horse Artillery Brigade							
Total at Trevilian Station, &c.*	9	98	32	438	8	427	1,007
White House (or Saint Peter's Church) and Black Creek (or Tansfall's Station), June 21, 1864.							
1st Maine E			1	5			6
9th New York		1	1	5			7
1st Pennsylvania		3		28	3	19	53
17th Pennsylvania		5		12			17
Total White House, &c		10	1	50	3	19	83
Saint Mary's Church, June 24, 1864.							
1st Maine	2	7	5	41	3	8	66
1st Massachusetts		1		2		2	5
1st New Jersey				1		2	3
10th New York	1			13	1	7	22
6th Ohio E		3	1	31			35
1st Pennsylvania	1	1	2	8	1	12	25
2d Pennsylvania			1	19	2	27	49
10th Pennsylvania	1	4		19	1	12	37
8th Pennsylvania		2		13	2	7	24
13th Pennsylvania		2		14	3	25	44
16th Pennsylvania		1		7		3	11
1st U. S. Artillery, Batteries H and I		2		10		4	16
2d U. S. Artillery, Battery A E		1		1			2
Total Saint Mary's Church†	5	24	9	179	13	109	339
Minor skirmishes, &c., en route, June 7-24, 1864.‡							
1st New Jersey						2	2
4th New York				1			1
6th New York		6	1	12	1	4	24
9th New York				2		2	4
10th New York		2		4		5	11
19th New York (1st Dragoons) E				2		2	4
6th Ohio						9	9
2d Pennsylvania				2		1	3
4th Pennsylvania						3	3
6th Pennsylvania						1	1
13th Pennsylvania				1			1
16th Pennsylvania		1		1		5	7
17th Pennsylvania				2		1	3
6th United States						7	7
1st U. S. Artillery, Batteries H and I				1			1
2d U. S. Artillery, Battery D						2	2
Grand total Trevilian raid	14	136	43	695	25	599	1,512

Officers killed or mortally wounded.—Col. William Sackett, 9th New York; Capts. Alpheus W. Carr, 1st Michigan, John Ordner, 10th New York, and Albert C. Walker (killed June 10), 2d Pennsylvania; Lieuts. Robert S. Warren, 1st Michigan, Oliver S. Wood, 4th New York, John H. Nichols and Frederick C. Ogden, 1st United States, Michael Lawless, 2d United States, Joseph P. Henley, 5th United States, and Philip D. Mason, 1st U. S. Artillery.

† *Officers killed or mortally wounded.*—Capts. Walstein Phillips and Osco A. Ellis, 1st Maine; Lieut. Henry M. Baldwin, 6th Ohio; Lieuts. Alonzo Reed and Joseph S. Wright, 1st Pennsylvania; Col. George H. Covode, 4th Pennsylvania; Capt. Wilkinson W. Paige, 10th New York.

‡ Including King and Queen Court-House, June 18 and 20; Jones' Bridge June 23 &c.

E Joined expedition during Sheridan's retreat.

By far the largest collector of military artifacts in this area is Elton H. Strong, Jr., of Mineral, Virginia. He has scoured the Battlefield of Trevilian Station with his metal detector and has amassed a room-full of bullets, buttons, cannon balls, buckles, bayonets, insignia, revolvers, guns, swords and other items too numerous to mention.

Among Strong's most interesting and prized articles are lead bullets with soldiers' teeth marks indented into the metal. These were found around buildings used as first aid stations or hospitals where men being operated on were given bullets to clench their teeth on when their arms or legs were being amputated.

The following photos show only a few of the hundreds of items in Elton H. Strong, Jr.'s museum of military collectables.

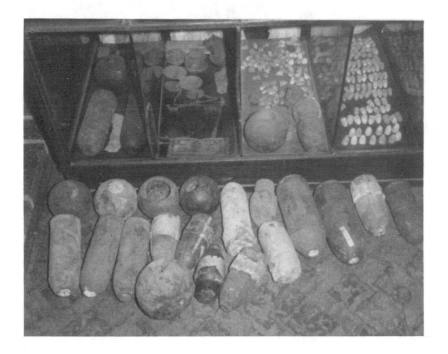

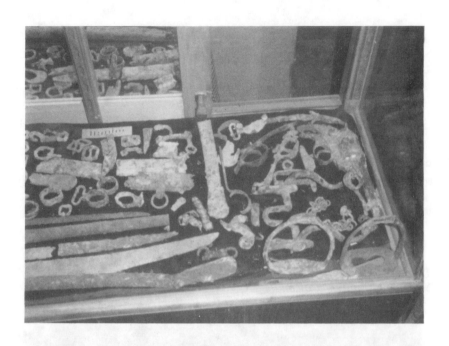

34

William H. Kiblinger of Mineral, Virginia, shows a Yankee cavalry sabre found by his uncle Hiram H. Kiblinger on his farm near the Dunn house across the railroad track from the Ogg house. This area was occupied by the First and Seventh Michigan Cavalry of Custer's Brigade on the final day of the Battle of Trevilian Station, Louisa County, Virginia, June 12, 1864 (see map on page 19).

The above exhibit in the Military Museum at West Point shows, left, the coat worn by General U.S. Grant after he was promoted to General of the Army in 1866. The two star shoulder insignia, upper left, was worn by Grant when he was promoted to Major General on July 4, 1863, upon his capture of Vicksburg.

At the upper right is the two star shoulder insignia worn by Major General Philip Sheridan at the surrender scene at Appomattox Court House.

The badge was that of Sheridan's Cavalry Corps.

Sheridan's sabre, worn at the Battle of Trevilians, is in the foreground.

In the upper portion of the above picture, taken at the Military Museum at West Point, is the sash worn by General Robert E. Lee at Appomattox Court House on April 9, 1865.

The frock coat was worn by Major General Thomas Rosser and was captured at Toms Brook in the Shenandoah Valley by troops under General George A. Custer, a friend and former West Point classmate of General Rosser. Custer, having received and subsequently worn the coat, wrote to Rosser that it fitted excellently, but it would suit him, Custer, better in ordering the next suit, if Rosser would have the coat made a trifle shorter in the tails.

The Confederate foot officer's sword shown in the picture was carried by Lieutenant Sam Smyth of the Third Georgia Infantry when he was killed at the Second Battle of Manassas in 1862.

Shown in the background in the above picture of an exhibit at the Military Museum at West Point is the Confederate Battle Flag of the Fifth South Carolina Cavalry captured at Trevilian Station by the Ninth New York Cavalry and presented to New York State by Major John Manly of the latter regiment.

In the foreground is the uniform coat, sash and forage cap worn by Lieutenant Colonel L. Hoxton, a Confederate Artillery Officer.

Also pictured are three Confederate rifles of various calibres.

At the instigation of the writer, Robert C. Brown, Commander of the General P.G.T. Beauregard Camp 1459, Sons of Confederate Veterans, Sumter, South Carolina, was able to have the Confederate Battle Flag of the Fifth South Carolina Cavalry returned to South Carolina.

Commander Brown is pictured, in the center, below with the flag at a ceremony held at the Confederate Relic Room and War Museum in Sumter, South Carolina. Ancestors of all three men in the picture fought in Company H of the Fifth South Carolina Cavalry.

Biographical Sketches of Commanders

Wade Hampton was the son and grandson of aristocratic and wealthy South Carolina planters. Throughout his life he was known as a mighty hunter, an avid fisherman, and was as renowned for his physical strength as he was for his mastery of the arts of woodcraft. He was born at Charleston in 1818 and after graduation from South Carolina College read law so he could better handle his own affairs. In the early 1850s he began to have doubts as to the economics of slave labor and entered the state legislature in order to counteract the radical proposals of many of his peers. He proved to be a worthy manager of his large estates in South Carolina and Mississippi, and his wealth (his father had sold his Louisiana lands for $1,500,000 in 1857, the year before his death) deservedly placed him in

General Wade Hampton

the forefront of the leaders of his state. When secession became imminent Hampton believed in the right of a state to secede yet doubted the advisability of such a policy. However, when the die was cast, he placed his wealth and his services at the command of the state.

He set about the formation of a legion, largely supported from his own pocket. In it were six companies of infantry, four of cavalry and a battery of six guns of the advanced and revolutionary Blakely type. Later when these units were found awkward and unwieldy to handle in a military organization the infantry was transferred to Hood's Texas Brigade, the cavalry became part of Rosser's Brigade and the artillery came to be known as Hart's South Carolina Battery and served with Hampton at Trevilians.

Although he had no formal military training Hampton was a man born to lead and throughout the war discharged his duties in an exemplary fashion. He was with Stuart in nearly all of his major engagements, and some time after the death of his leader commanded the cavalry corps of Lee's army, rising to the rank of Lieutenant General. His brother Frank was killed at Brandy Station and his son Preston at Burgess Mill.

After the war Hampton, like many of his fellow South Carolinians, found himself much reduced in circumstances. Twice was he elected governor of his state and in addition he served two terms in the United States Senate. His long and productive life came to an end in 1902.

General Fitzhugh Lee
Nephew of Robert E. Lee

Fitzhugh Lee, the oldest of six brothers, was born in 1835, his father being the elder brother of Robert E. Lee. He graduated from the Military Academy in 1856, but did not equal the record of his uncle ranking number 45 in a class of 49. Three years later he was dangerously wounded fighting Indians in Texas. For a few months in 1861 he was an instructor at West Point but resigned his commission in favor of service in the Confederate army. He saw much action in the war and perhaps his outstanding feat was the guarding of Jackson's march around Hooker's right wing at Chancellorsville. It was he who discovered that the right of Howard's XI Corps was in the air and by reason of his reconnaissance, Jackson made the necessary dispositions for his devastating and decisive attack. He commanded a division under Stuart and after the death of that leader was junior to Wade Hampton. General R.E. Lee exhibited concern whether this would cause dissension between his trusted cavalry lieutenants, but if Fitz Lee was disappointed he covered his feelings well and his service was commended by Hampton. In the Shenandoah Valley on July 19, 1864, Lee had three horses shot under him and was severely wounded.

Rejoining the army in January 1865, he fought through the final months of the war and at Appomattox, refusing to surrender, rode off with a part of his command. By April 11, however, realizing that further resistance was futile, he surrendered at Farmville.

Lee was respected as a good tactician, hard-hitting and skillful at reconnaissance, but he lacked the strategical sense of a Forrest or a Stuart. Freeman refers to him as a "Laughing Cavalier", but pays tribute to him as a serious and competent fighter. The long and luxuriant beard he affected added years to the appearance of a young man who as a major general at the age of twenty-eight.

After the war he returned to farming and was elected Governor of Virginia in 1885. As Consul General at Havana he handled his post with tact and skill in the difficult period prior to the Spanish-American War. Later, as Major General in the United States Army, he commanded the force occupying Cuba. Lee died in 1905.

Matthew Calbraith Butler, born in 1836 in Greenville, graduated from South Carolina College and then studied law. His father, a naval surgeon and his mother, sister of Oliver Hazzard Perry, had sixteen children of which the future general was the eleventh. He married the daughter of Governor F.W. Pickens. His service began when he resigned his seat in the state legislature and accepted a commission as captain in Hampton's Legion. He lost his right foot at Brandy Station, a victim of the same shell that killed the famous scout Farley. A veteran of all the campaigns of the Army of Northern Virginia, he was granted his second star in September, 1864. He spent the last months of the war with Johnston facing Sherman in North

General Matthew C. Butler

Carolina. Later he was a lawyer, legislator, and served three terms in the United States Senate. He died in 1909 having also served in the United States Army as a major general during the war with Spain.

Butler has not received the acclaim accorded to more flamboyant cavalry leaders but a study of his record reveals that his performance was always on a high level and he earned the respect and regard of such men as R.E. Lee, Stuart and Hampton. Butler was a handsome and graceful man, brave and cool under fire and had a reputation for carrying no weapons in battle, but led his men with only a silver mounted riding whip in his hand.

General Thomas L. Rosser

Thomas Lafayette Rosser's life span nearly paralleled that of General Butler, but whereas both men were born in the same year, Rosser outlived his companion by a single year. Rosser was born in Virginia but when thirteen moved with his family to Texas, from which state he was appointed to the Military Academy in the class of '61. He resigned before graduation and joined the Washington Artillery in time to fight at the first Bull Run. He was wounded during the Peninsula Campaign and on his recovery returned to the army as Colonel of the Fifth Virginia Cavalry. As commander of the Laurel Brigade he defeated his good friend and ex-classmate Custer at Buckland Mills in October, 1863. The rivalry of Rosser versus Custer was renewed at Trevilians and again during the last days of Lee's army. Disdaining surrender at Appomattox he led his command in a charge through encircling Union lines but was captured May 2 near Hanover Court House.

In later life Rosser was one of the most successful of the surviving Confederate leaders. He rose to the position of Chief Engineer of the Northern Pacific Railroad and in the Indian Territory, where Custer was protecting the railroad construction crews, he resumed his friendship with his earlier adversary. From 1881 to 1886, Rosser was Chief Engineer of the Canadian Pacific Railroad. Later, having profited from wise investments in real estate, he purchased "Rugby" in Charlottesville and became a gentleman farmer. In 1905 he was appointed postmaster in that city. Until his death he was one of the best liked and most respected men in the community. In his prime he was six feet two inches in height and endowed with extraordinary strength and endurance.

It was Rosser's misfortune to be host to Pickett and Fitz Lee at the ill-fated shad bake at a time that Sheridan was shattering the Confederate defenses at Five Forks.

Lunsford Lindsay Lomax, a descendant of an old Virginia family, was born in 1835 at Newport, Rhode Island, where his father, a captain in the United States Artillery, was stationed. He graduated from the Military Academy with his close friend, Fitz Lee, ranking twenty-first in his class, but resigned his commission in April, 1861. In the early years of the war he saw service in Arkansas, Mississippi, Louisiana and Tennessee. He returned east in time to lead the Eleventh Virginia Cavalry at Gettysburg and was appointed general the same month. Lomax served with Stuart's corps until transferred to the Shenandoah Valley in the late summer of 1864. He and his troops joined Johnston in North Carolina and surrendered with him in April, 1865.

General Lunsford L. Lomax

After the war Lomax farmed in Warrenton and became president of what is now Virginia Polytechnic Institute. He resigned in 1899 and moved to Washington where he assisted in the compilation of that massive work, the "Official Records". He was also a commissioner of the Gettysburg National Park. He died in 1913, the last but one of the surviving Confederate generals.

William Carter Wickham was born in 1820 at Richmond, educated at the University of Virginia, practiced law, ran his plantation and found time to be a legislator, a jurist and a militiaman. Although opposing the ordinance of secession, he fought at First Bull Run. He received a severe sabre wound at Williamsburg and spent the rest of the Peninsula campaign convalescing. During this period he was captured and exchanged for a relative of his wife. He commanded his brigade through all of the engagements of the Army of Northern Virginia until he resigned his general's

General William Carter Wickham

commission in November of 1864, at which time he assumed the congressional seat to which he had been elected shortly after the battle of Chancellorsville.

He joined the Republican party in April of 1865, an act that exposed him to much personal criticism, although it did not appear to hamper his business career, which was outstanding. He served as president of the Virginia Central Railroad and later of the Chesapeake and Ohio. In 1890 he declined President Hayes' offer of appointment as Secretary of the Navy, and a year later he likewise declined the Republican nomination for governor. From 1883 until his death five years later, he again served in the state senate. Despite Wickham's politics, which were highly erratic in the opinion of his associates, a statue of him stands in the grounds of the state capital at Richmond.

Major General Philip Sheridan and staff. Left to right: Sheridan, Generals George A. Forsythe, Wesley Merritt, Thomas C. Devin and George A. Custer. Inset upper left: David McM. Gregg. Upper right: Alfred T.A. Torbert.

Philip Henry Sheridan was born in Albany, New York, in 1831 of Irish parents who had come to this country the previous year. Shortly after the birth of their son, the family moved to Ohio from which state Philip was appointed to the Military Academy. He graduated in 1853, not, however, without displaying some of the characteristics which marked his later years. In the fall of 1851,

Sheridan received an order from his Cadet Sergeant which he considered to have been made in an improper tone, and responded to it by making for the sergeant, a Virginia cadet, W.R. Terrell. He restrained himself before physical contact was made, but Terrell, as was his duty, reported the incident. Sheridan was so incensed by this action that when he next saw Terrell in front of barracks he attacked him. The resulting fight was stopped by an officer, and Sheridan was forced to leave the Academy for a year. Thus he graduated a year behind his class and his standing, 34th in a class of 52 due to the incident, was such that he could not secure a preferred appointment. When the war broke out he was a comparatively old lieutenant and filled several administrative posts before securing a field command. He was made Colonel of the Second Michigan Cavalry on May 25, 1862, and won his first general's star at Boonesville on July 1st of the same year. He was promoted to major general in December of 1862. He further distinguished himself in the Chattanooga campaign and came east as commander of the Cavalry Corps of the Army of the Potomac. In accordance with Grant's recommendation and despite his youth (he was thirty-three) he was appointed commander of the Middle Military District, which included the Shenandoah Valley, in August, 1864. His effective campaign in the Valley cut off all Confederate supplies from this area and ended military action west of the Blue Ridge. Sheridan rejoined the Army of the Potomac for the Appomattox campaign, his victory at Five Forks and vigorous pursuit of Lee contributing no little to the final outcome.

After the war Sheridan was military governor in Louisiana, and so severe was his rule that he was recalled half a year later. After observing the Franco-Prussian War of 1870, he returned to Louisiana in 1875 to subdue political disturbances and again found himself in trouble because of his severity. In 1884 he succeeded Sherman as Commander in Chief of the Army and, in 1888, not long before he died, he received his fourth star.

Sheridan was short (two inches under Grant's five feet seven inches), black haired, square shouldered and squat. His temper was extremely uncertain, and, unlike Grant, his tongue was not unacquainted with profanity. At times he was extremely harsh with his subordinates, his treatment of General G.K. Warren at Five Forks being an outstanding example. To many, the lack of generosity in Sheridan toward that able and devoted officer after the heat of battle had cooled, was unpardonable. Warren died, as one biographer has said, "of a broken heart" in 1882, only nine months after a court of inquiry published its findings exonerating him from the major charges of dilatory personal leadership. Sheridan was a hard man, but a man who got things done.

Alfred Thomas Archimedes Torbert had a military record as long and distinguished as his name. He was appointed to the Military Academy from Delaware and graduated 21st of a class of 34 in 1855. He saw service on the frontier, fought against the Seminoles and marched in the Utah expedition. During the Civil War he first served as an infantry officer before being transferred to the cavalry in April of 1864. He commanded the First Division, Cavalry Corps, Army of the Potomac, later fought in the Shenandoah Valley and for a time commanded the Army of the Shenandoah. He achieved the rank of Major General and retired in 1866 to enter the consular service. After holding posts in Salvador, Havana and Paris, he entered business in Mexico. In 1880 he was drowned in a shipwreck off the Florida coast while en route to Mexico.

It could be said that Torbert was not as successful when he was in overall command as he was while subordinate to another commander. As a division commander he was dependable, a hard fighter and a leader respected and followed by his men.

David McMurtrie Gregg, a native of Pennsylvania, graduated eighth of the thirty-four members of the class of 1855 at West Point. In 1861 he came east after six years of Indian fighting and was named Captain of the Third United States Cavalry. Promotion came to him rapidly as he showed unquestioned ability in the major engagements of the Army of the Potomac. He received much credit at Gettysburg, where on July 3rd he repulsed Stuart's attempt to turn Meade's flank and attack the Union rear.

Gregg resigned from the army on February 3, 1865, holding the brevet rank of Major General. For the remainder of his long life he lived in Pennsylvania, much respected for his modesty, geniality and ability. He was considered by Grant to be one of the best cavalry officers in the army, although he was never held in high esteem by Sheridan, that officer considering him to be too precise and gentlemanly to be a successful cavalryman.

In his command, Sheridan had several outstanding brigade commanders: Merritt, Devin, Davies and Gregg. Wesley Merritt, after outstanding service in the war, served as commander of the Military Academy, led the first Philippine expedition in 1898, and with Admiral Dewey received the surrender of Manila. Thomas Devin, a painter by trade, and not a West Pointer, rose to the rank of Major General, U.S. Volunteers, during the war and remained in the regular army until his death in 1878, at which time he was Colonel of the Third U.S. Cavalry. In his late thirties when the war started, Devin was considerably older than most of the cavalry leaders, but age was no handicap to his abilities, and he was considered one of the best.

Henry Davies attended Harvard and Williams before graduating from Columbia and practiced law until he was commissioned in May of 1861. He advanced to division command in 1864, resigned from the army in 1866, and returning to the law, held several public offices. He authored a biography of General Sheridan and several other books. Not trained to the military life, he nevertheless mastered his new profession thoroughly. General Rodenbough described him as "unpolished, genial, gallant".

John Irvin Gregg, a Mexican War veteran, was a captain in the regular cavalry when the war broke out. Three times wounded, he commanded a brigade in almost all the engagements in the east. He was captured at Farmville and released three days later on Lee's surrender. He continued in the army, retiring in 1879 as Colonel of the Eighth Cavalry.

In addition to these officers of undenied ability, Sheridan also had George Armstrong Custer with him. For many years Custer has remained an enigma to historians, and it is doubtful whether the mystery of his character will ever be resolved. He was born in New Rumley, Ohio, on December 5, 1839. His paternal grandfather, a Hessian officer named Küster, surrendered with Burgoyne at Saratoga and later settled in Pennsylvania and Maryland. Custer graduated from West Point in 1861, and had the dubious distinction of ranking 34th in a class of 34. As a newly commissioned second lieutenant, he served at Bull Run, arriving on the field the morning of the battle. It was not until June, 1863 that Custer received his first brigade command, a group of Michigan cavalry regiments. In the early days of the war, his dress had been slovenly and unkempt, but when he became a general a transformation took place. Colonel Kidd, commander of one of Custer's regiments, describes his first sight of his general. "Looking at him closely, this is what I saw: An officer, superbly mounted, who sat his charger as if to the manner born. Tall, lithe, active, muscular, straight as an Indian and as quick in his movements, he had the fair complexion of a schoolgirl. He was clad in a suit of black velvet, elaborately trimmed with gold lace, which ran down the outer seams of his trousers, and almost covered the sleeves of his cavalry jacket. The wide collar of a navy-blue shirt was turned down over the collar of his velvet jacket, and a necktie of brilliant crimson was tied in a graceful knot at the throat, the long ends falling carelessly in front. The double rows of buttons on his breast were arranged in groups of twos, indicating the rank of brigadier-general. A soft black hat with wide brim adorned with a gilt cord, and rosette encircling a silver star, was worn turned down on one side, giving him a rakish air. His golden hair fell in graceful luxuriance nearly or quite to his shoulder, and his upper lip was garnished with a blonde mustache. A sword and belt, gilt spurs and top-boots completed his unique outfit.''

His energy, flair for the dramatic and the almost unvarying success of his operations made him a popular and much relied on commander. There was no question of his personal bravery; he had had twelve horses killed under him during the war and usually could be found in the middle of a melee, slashing with his sabre, alongside his men. His performance during the final pursuit of Lee capped his brilliant wartime record. His division held the van and day after day, stopping seldom for food or sleep, kept boring into Lee's shrinking forces until early on April 9, 1865, he blocked Gordon's road and made further resistance useless. It was to Custer that the Confederate flag of truce was brought. His commander, Sheridan, wrote of him, ''I know of no one whose efforts have contributed more to this happy result than those of Custer.''

His subsequent career is even better known than the achievements of his war years. Reduced in rank after the war, as were many others, he reverted to Captain of the Fifth Cavalry. The next few years were stormy for Custer and those around him, and culminated with his death at the Little Big Horn in 1876, when he was only thirty-six.

He did not smoke and except for a brief period during the war did not drink. He was a man about whom no one could be neutral. He won devoted friends, but he also made vindictive enemies, particularly among his brother officers. Custer could exude considerable personal charm and in his later days became an avid scholar and spent much of his spare time writing. In 1874 his narrative, ''My Life on the Plains'' was published and after his death his ''War Memoirs'' came out.

Capturing the Yankees

The following is a story about an interesting event that happened just before the Battle of Trevilians.

Dr. Joe Baker was at his home recuperating from a severe wound he received at Spottsylvania courthouse on the 12th of May, having practically recovered after a month's careful nursing at home. A rumor reached him that the Yankees were coming. The next morning a cloud of dust was seen at Carpenter's Ford, where the enemy were crossing the river, and he realized that he must make his escape. The question arose how he might get a weapon out of the house without arousing the suspicion of his mother, who was in an extremely nervous condition, and in the end he had to get away without a weapon of any kind.

Dr. Baker went about a mile down the road and told the two young Powell boys, Rupert and Hawes, and they got an old gun for him and accompanied him through the pines to Bibb's Store.

All of this time the Yankees were in the neighborhood of Bibb's Store, and Dr. Baker accompanied by the two boys were overtaken at Gold Mine Church and were obliged to find refuge in the woods. Dr. Baker says he hid behind a fallen log, and in plain view all of Sheridan's Army passed by. He told the boys to watch the road while he went to see if any had stopped at Woolfolk's Store. A minute later the boys whistled and returning to the place he had left he saw three Yankees riding up the road. He waited concealed until they got close to him, then he threw up his gun and ordered them to surrender. They seemed disposed to do so, seeing that he was alone, and started to make a move that would give them a chance to take a shot at him, but he called to the boys and succeeded in making them unbuckle their six shooters, sabres and carbines and took their horses from them. The prisoners were carried to Mr. Massie's home and Dr. Baker and the two boys walked them to the Courthouse, where they were turned over to the authorities.

A Confederate Soldier

The following poem was written March 22, 1910 by Edmond Fontain of Charlottesville, Virginia. He was a descendant of a Beaverdam family in Hanover County. His ancestor was Edward Fontaine, a wartime President of the Virginia Central Railroad.

A soldier sad, with bended back,
And hardly hair, and years of wrack;
Beneath the oak tree by his door
He fighteth his many battles o'er:
— Shall I tell you Son, how them Yankees run
At the first Manassas battle
And we give them Hell, with shot and shell —
Stampeded 'em like cattle.

His aged eye has the fire of Youth,
His palsied hands are strong with Truth,
The words sound weird, as from the dead,
So list ye now to what he said:
— Yes, I was there, when the trumpets blare
Sent us on at the double-quick,
And we went at the wall, as they go to a ball,
The boys were falling thick.

His vibrant voice sounds rich and clear,
As he tells of his Youth, to Memory dear;
His eyes flash fire, tho his frame is frail,
As he charges again thru the leaden hail:
— The Bloody Angle was a terrible tangle,
And I fell right close to the fence:
Some did not survive, but you see I'm alive,
Tho his quite frequently sence.

He speaks of Jeb Stuart, so handsome and gay,
And Hampton and Munford who knew not Dismay,
Brave Gentlemen all, who warred like men,
Tho the Foe were but burners of Homes and Farm Pen.
— So he talks of the Past — such Ideals will last
When bigoted Hate is forgotten,
And Time yet to be, shall set us all free,
For Freedom of Truth is begotten.

He seizes his stick, and sweareth by Rosser
Who rescued Fitz Lee at Trevillian,
And the sound of the sabres ring clear and sharp,
For the Vet'ran is fighting a million:
— Jackson and Lee, and the Foot-cavalry
Were men of a caliber large,
And they made old Joe Hooker, such a comical looker
— Living at Bank's charge.

A pensionless Patriot, poor but possest
With Wealth which is better than Gold — a bequest
To his Son and the Nation, and men of all time,
His Honour and Manhood, and Faith most sublime.
— So read you this rhyme, to those of your Time,
Who best love the Truth, and a Man
Like Robert E. Lee, who held his Duty
To be better than Place or Plan.

A soldier sad, with bended back,
And hoary hair, and years of wrack;
Beneath the oak tree by his door
He fighteth his many battles o'er.
— So we leave him there, with Comforts rare,
And his Comrades where they be:
Fate gave them not, the Victory sweet,
But Immortality.

Edmond Fontaine

March 23rd, 1910   Charlottesville, Virginia

A Letter of Despair

When the guns of the North and South ceased to fire in the early spring of 1865, the citizens of Louisa County, like those throughout the Southland, faced devastation, poverty, loss of property, civil and economic restrictions and despair. This is so well reflected in the following letter from Colonel Claybrook, who lived in Brookville (Frederick's Hall), to his brother in Tennessee, written May 1, 1866—a year after Appomattox.

Dear Brother:

I received your acceptable letter yesterday. It gives us great pleasure to hear from you and to find you are in comfortable circumstances. It would be impossible for me to give you a detailed account of my life for the last four years. We have been visited three times by Northern raiders. The new part of our house (old now) was General Merrit's headquarters and we were reduced to the necessity of taking supper with him. They left us no corn, meat, oats or fodder. They left us without food. They killed nearly all of my hogs and some of the cattle and sheep, but did not burn anything except fence rails and plank and such things. Some of his men threatened to burn the house the last raid they ransacked the house from bottom to top. General Sheridan occupied Dr. Pendleton's and General Custer Frederickshall house. I assure you the people around here were in a bad fix. I had to borrow corn for bread and the horses had to work on grass. I had no money at that time and I found a friend quite acceptable. Some houses they did not visit at all. The neighborhood of J. Hart's escaped. I am better off at this time. I have sold about 75 acres of land for the purpose of paying my debts and taxes. I think that you had better come to Virginia and live with us the rest of your life. Your time as well as mine is quite agreeable to the course of nature, either of us have scarcely time to tell our tale of the last four years. You must come to see us and talk over things anyhow. I have no labour only by the month and day. An experiment which I do not think will answer. Some of our people, I for one, have gone into partnership and some have both B. and white tenants. Our brother John called on me last summer. He looks well and from his account there is not much difference in different parts of the South and West. Sallie sends love and mine also. You have not anything to prevent you from coming to see us.

Your affectionately,

There is little wonder, after reading such letters, that the South was bitter. A less virile race would have given up in despair; no money, no teams, no farm implements, no fences; as Shakespeare says of the old man, "sans everything".

Chapter III

EYEWITNESSES TO THE
BATTLE OF TREVILIAN STATION

---

*Nothing can surpass the words
of the man who was there!*

A. BRIGADIER GENERAL MATTHEW C. BUTLER, C.S.A.

Butler's Brigade, Hampton's Division, Cavalry Corps, ANVA

Below are the remarks of Major General Matthew C. Butler, who commanded his Brigade at the Battle of Trevilian Station, Virginia. He magnificently supported Major General Wade Hampton in defeating Union Major General Philip Sheridan in this greatest all cavalry engagement of the war.

"June 11, 1864

I rode from Netherland's toward Clayton's Store, on a road that I was picketing, for the purpose of reconnaissance.

We had advanced but a short distance from the railroad when we were met by Captain Mulligan's squadron, of the 4th South Carolina, which had been on picket, retiring before the enemy, by whom he had just been driven in. General Hampton then ordered me to bring up my brigade and attack at once, telling me that he was expecting to hear Fitzhugh Lee's guns on my right on his way up by another road from Louisa Court House. I sent in Captain Snowden's Squadron of the 4th South Carolina to charge whatever he met, and develop the force in front of us. It was soon ascertained that a heavy column of Sheridan's command was moving on us, and I thereupon dismounted squadron after squadron until my entire command was on foot, except Captain John C. Calhoun's squadron of the 4th South Carolina regiment, and we were soon driving the enemy before us in the very thick woods. I heard firing on my right and expected every moment to form a junction with Fitzhugh Lee.

While we were thus struggling with a superior force in my front, and the stubborn fight had been kept up at close quarters for several hours, I received information from the rear that Custer, with a mounted column, had moved by an open road to my right, around my right flank, and had captured some of my ambulances, whereupon I received orders from General Hampton to withdraw and mount my command. This was easier said than done...

"June 12, 1864

This morning General Hampton placed me in command of his division. The command of my brigade devolved upon Colonel Rutledge.

Colonel Aiken had been seriously wounded in the engagement of the day before.

Early in the afternoon I posted the division on the railroad near Denny's house, a mile above Trevilian Station. The line formed an obtuse angle on the railroad embankment, and extended off to the right with an open field in front, and to the left along the embankment. Beginning at the railroad, I had thrown up temporary breastworks of fence rails and such material as were available. Two batteries of horse artillery of four guns each—Hart's and Thomson's—stationed at convenient points along the line. In this position I awaited Sheridan's attack. Between 1 and 2 o'clock P.M. I was advised of his advance. He drove in my skirmishers, and moved promptly upon that portion of his line occupied by Rutledge with my brigade. This attack was repulsed without much effort. The second attack was made with much more vigor, and was directed sharply upon the angle above described, where the 6th South Carolina was stationed. This, too, was repulsed; and between then and dark five distinct and determined assaults were made upon us, making seven in all. Between sunset and dark, when the dusk of the evening was still further shrouded by the smoke of the battle, and after six assaults had been repulsed, we heard the usual preparation of another, and, as I concluded, the last desperate effort. I directed Major Chew to reman the two howitzers and double-shot them with canister, as I believed the enemy would emerge from the woods a little more than a stone's throw in our front, across the fence (which they had previously done), and rush our line. They did just as I had anticipated, and came charging out of the woods into the open field and into the railroad cut immediately in our front. Before the canister and the still steady fire of our carbines and rifles the enemy fell back for the last time before the deadly aim of our troops.

At the time Sheridan's sharp-shooters occupied houses just across the railroad in our immediate front, and kept up a destructive fire upon us from their sheltered position.

I directed the guns be turned upon them, and in a short time they set fire to the house where most of the enemy was gathered and the house was set on fire.

We had been engaged in this bloody encounter from its beginning without food or rest for either men or horses, in the broiling sun of a hot June day, and recuperation was absolutely necessary. As it was, I was not relieved and did not withdraw from my line until 2 o'clock on the morning of the 13th, and in the meantime had to care for the wounded and bury the dead.''

B. MAJOR GENERAL WADE HAMPTON, C.S.A.

Commanding Cavalry Corps, ANVA

The following is a report of Major General Wade Hampton, Commander, Cavalry Corps, Army of Northern Virginia, pertaining to the second day's battle at Trevilian Station.

"At 3:30 P.M. (12th) a heavy attack was made on my left where Butler's Brigade was posted. Being repulsed, the enemy made a succession of determined assaults, which were all handsomely repulsed. In the meantime General Lee had, by my direction, reenforced my left with General Wickham's Brigade, while he took General Lomax's across the Gordonsville road so as to strike the enemy on his right flank. This movement was successful, and the enemy, who had been heavily punished in front, when attacked on his flank fell back in confusion. I immediately gave orders to follow him up, but it was daylight before these orders could be carried out, the fight not being ended until 10 P.M."

C. BRIGADIER GENERAL THOMAS L. ROSSER, C.S.A.

Rosser's Brigade, Hampton's Division, ANVA

The following is a report of Brigadier General Thomas L. Rosser who commanded his Brigade at the Battle of Trevilian Station, Virginia.

"June 30, 1864

After I had dismounted my brigade about two miles west of Trevilian Station and was waiting to hear from scouts which I had sent out around the right flank of the enemy to ascertain if he were moving toward Gordonsville, a trooper from Young's brigade came galloping up from the rear with a saber cut across his face, and reported that the enemy had gotten in the rear of Young's and Butler's brigades, which were fighting on foot, and had captured the division wagon train and the horses of the dismounted men of these two brigades. I ordered a company to mount and go back and see if this report were true, but before it started off, several more men from the same command came running at full speed, yelling 'Yankees! Yankees!' I then mounted the brigade at once and riding at the head of it went back at a brisk trot in the direction whence these men had come.

Scrub oaks, almost a 'chaparall,' covered the ground on each side of the narrow road, and as the road was very crooked, I could not see a stone's throw ahead of me, and, expecting to find the enemy at or near the station, I was as much surprised as he appeared to be, when, turning a sharp curve in the road, I came immediately on him. It was Custer's brigade, which had passed around Butler's right between him and Fitzhugh Lee, had gotten in the rear of the former and captured the wagon train and the horses of the two brigades then fighting on foot. Not expecting trouble from the direction from which I came, Custer had not taken the precaution of putting pickets on that road, and thinking when he saw the head of my column that it was only a scouting party, he wheeled so as to meet the charge which I sounded on the sight of him; but I was too quick and too strong for him, and as I went crashing into him, breaking up and scattering his squadrons, he made a gallant and manly effort to resist me. Sitting on his horse in the midst of his advanced platoons, and near enough to be easily recognized by me, he encouraged and inspired his men by appeal as well as by example. His color-sergeant was shot down at his side, by Major Holmes Conrad, of my staff, when Custer grabbed the staff to save his flag, but the death-grip of the sergeant would not release it, so, with a quick jerk, Custer tore the flag from

59

its staff and in triumph carried it off. Closely pursuing, I recaptured our men, horses and wagons, as well as many prisoners from the enemy, and drove Custer back, with heavy losses, into Sheridan's lines."

In his fight General Rosser suffered a painful leg wound and General Hampton appointed one of Rosser's officers, Colonel Richard Dulany, Commanding the Seventh Virginia Cavalry, to command the Laurel Brigade in the absence of the injured Rosser.

D. BRIGADIER GENERAL THEO. F. RODENBOUGH, U.S.A.

Formerly Captain, Second U.S. Cavalry
Merritt's Brigade, First Division, Cavalry Corps, Army of the Potomac

The remarks below are those of Brigadier Theo. F. Rodenbough of the United States Army, who, as Captain, commanded the Second U.S. Cavalry Regiment, Reserve Brigade, First Division of Union General Philip Sheridan's Corps at the Battle of Trevilian Station.

"Part of (General) Hampton's force attacked (General) Custer, killing some of the men and horses of (Lieutenant) Pennington's battery before it could gallop into a more favorable position and open on the enemy. Colonel Alger, 5th Michigan Cavalry, got in between Hampton's dismounted men and their led horses, capturing about 350 men and horses. Custer sent his captures to the rear,—that is toward Louisa Court House,—where also were parked his wagons and the caissons of Penningtin's battery. It was then supposed that Hampton's entire force was in their front. It appears, however, that (General) Fitz Lee, who should have been closed up on Hampton, was late in getting out that morning, and Custer, without knowing it, struck the road between them. When Lee attempted to close up he espied a wagon-train, caissons, etc., (Custer's), and obligingly took them under his protection. The spoil included all of Custer's captures, (except two hundred prisoners), his headquarters wagon, and his colored cook, 'Eliza,' who usually occupied an antique ruin of a family carriage on the march, and was called by the soldiers 'the Queen of Sheba.' In the fluctuations of the fight that day 'the Queen' escaped and came into camp with her employer's valise, which she had managed to secure."

E.   COLONEL A.C.M. PENNINGTON, U.S.A.

Formerly Lieutenant, Second U.S. Battery M, Horse Artillery Cavalry Corps, Army of the Potomac

The comments below are those of Colonel A.C.M. Pennington of the U.S. Army, who, as a Lieutenant, commanded Horse Battery "M", Second U.S. Artillery at the Battle of Trevilian Station, Virginia, June 11-12, 1864.

"June 11, 1864

We moved out about 6:30 A.M., the battery following the leading regiment. As the command struck the road we discovered the impedimenta of a cavalry column, packmules, ambulances, wagons, etc., all of which we captured and sent to our rear a short distance. The enemy, which turned out to be Hampton's division going toward Gordonsville ahead of us, halted and began to form. I was ordered to bring two guns forward to a position selected by General Custer; found Custer at a high board-fence, which separated him from the station (Trevilian). He told me to bring one gun on the road and bring the other to where he stood with his staff, mounted. I took up the gun and placed it in position, pointing at the board-fence, from which we were to knock the boards to enable us to enfilade a battery of the enemy. Number one at the gun had his axe uplifted in the act of striking, when we discovered a line of dismounted rebel cavalry getting over a rail-fence, about a hundred yards on our right. Custer ordered every one 'to get out of there,'—and we lost no time."

—Colonel A.C.M. Pennington

NOTE: See remarks of Sergeant John Gill, Chapter IIIN., in which he states that he was in the charge that broke General Custer's line at the Battle of Trevilian Station and captured Pennington's Headquarters wagons and Horse Artillery. His trophy in the affair was a handsome buffalo robe taken from the officer's wagon.

F. LIEUTENANT WILEY C. HOWARD

Commander, Co. C, Cobb Legion (Georgia)
Young's Brigade, Hampton's Division, ANVA

Wiley C. Howard

"On the morning of the first day of the Battle of Trevilian Station, the 11th of June 1864, I was suffering with a severe throat trouble and under advice of Dr. H.S. Bradley, our surgeon, I remained with the led horses, the command fighting dismounted and driving back the enemy in front; but a body of Sheridan's force somehow came in our rear and a stampede occurred with the led horses. Mounted on a horse of one of our dead comrades, I did what I could to stay the rush; but the Seventh Georgia being driven back on us, a general fall-back and reforming of the lines was necessary and in the melee I was chased for a mile by fifty or more Yankees. I jumped my horse over a pile of shells spilled in the road by a disabled caison. Finally, my horse, descending a slant, stumbled and fell. I caught on my hands, tearing the hide from my hand and exposing the leaders. As I ran, a Yankee overtook me, shooting and shouting 'Surrender,' but I did not. I scrambled over the fence and heard a ball hit the rail behind me. I made time across the field while the whole pack practiced on me as a target. Strange to say, I was not hit and soon gained the cover of a wood, worn down and panting. Pushing ahead, I stumbled on an old citizen in hiding with his favorite mare and soon ran onto a Jeff Davis Legion man who was having an experience similar to mine. I did not see him till he confronted me with a pistol ready to fire, as he mistook me for an enemy. We were soon reconciled and agreed to stick together in our perils. Fearing, from sounds of fighting, etc., that the enemy would be upon us, we slipped down the head of a branch in a swamp and hid in thick alder bushes at the head of an old pond, which was shortly after skirted by Yankees, as we could tell, peeping through the thick foliage and listening to their curses and imprecation on rebels. While they remained in the vicinity it seemed an age, as we persevered profound silence and my throat grew worse so that I could not suppress a cough and Hopkins, my fellow sufferer and companion in suspense and trouble, would force his canteen into my mouth as each spasm of coughing came on, until the enemy had gone away. We feared to come out, as we might run into a squad of the foe instead of our own men. So after prolonged conference and debate in low tones, we planned how we might succeed in getting back within our own lines, even if we had to wait till night and either elude the vigilance of the enemy's picket or, if need be, surprise and silence one, while we together mounted his steed and rode to safety and liberty in Dixie, rather than endure a Yankee prison. As a precautionary measure, I buried in the mud a pack of very precious and splendidly written love letters from my Virginia sweetheart I had treasured, and some from my sisters too, in case I could not escape the clutches of the enemy. It cost a pang to part with them, but they were too sacred to be exposed to the vulgar gaze of the ruthless foe and hawked about with gibes and merciless ribaldry. Then, concealing as best I could some Confederate money and my watch in my clothing, I persuaded my comrade to attempt a reconnoiter, and we stealthily crept down stream until in view of a mound. I crawled up on it and listening to the din of battle and watching the clouds of dust, I thought I comprehended the situation and we could rejoin our command. With some difficulty, by signalling him up from the brush, I persuaded Hopkins to join me and when he had surveyed the scene, he at length agreed to my suggestion of how to approach and ascertain the situation. So down the stream we hastened until I could discern enough to strengthen my notion that we were near our provost guard, who were corralling a lot of Yankee prisoners. So we leaped the fence and running a mile I found I was right and to our joy we were again with our own men. Lieut. Moke Simmons, whose widow still lives in Atlanta, was in command of the guard and a hundred and fifty or two hundred prisoners. He was a good fellow and learning briefly of my experience and the loss of my horse, he promptly proposed to mount me. So calling a Yankee Lieut. Colonel who was still mounted on his horse, he introduced me. I told him that I regretted the circumstances of war which made it necessary for me to deprive him of his mount. He was a gentleman and with a salute dismounted, pleasantly remarking that such were the fortunes of war and further that his horse was government property and not his, he courteously handed me the reins. By tearing strips from my shirt tail with the aid of those about me, I got my scalped wrist, which I had bandaged before with my handkerchief, into a sling so as to make it more comfortable and mounted my new Yankee horse with Simmons' aid. In spite of his entreaties to remain with him, as I was unfit to go to the front, on the fighting line, I rode rapidly towards the front, hoping in some way to find my lost horse and English tree-saddle and saddle bags, containing a new suit of jeans lately received from home. As I approached nearer where the fighting was going on, I suddenly came upon Gen. Hampton debouching from a by-way into the main road, who stopped me and inquired concerning my morning experience, etc. He told me to stay with him, as he had just sent away all his couriers and it would be some time before members of his staff could find him after carrying orders to different parts of the line. He proceeded towards the front to a point he had expected to meet certain of his staff, and as they and the couriers came, most of them were quickly sent again with other messages, and I held his horse while he read brief notes and wrote others to be dispatched. The day was wearing away and Hampton had largely regained the ground occupied in the morning. Wounded men and some prisoners were being taken to the rear. At length, when he had sent all his aids away, he asked me if I could deliver a verbal message to Gen. Rosser and, giving me directions as to the location of Rosser's brigade, I put my Yankee steed on his metal and after a time came upon the brigade hotly engaged dismounted. It was powerful uncomfortable where I found Rosser, but I was bound to go to him unless bullets stopped me. When I delivered my message, that gallant commander and superb fighter said, 'Give the general my compliments and tell him we are giving 'em hell.' I need not say I rode swiftly away, for it was hot and uncomfortable and I hastened to rejoin our chief who had then been rejoined by staff officers and moved in another direction and nearer a portion of the line. When I saluted and delivered Rosser's message, Hampton snapped his eyes, smiled and said to the staff, 'General Rosser is a magnificent fighter and has done much to turn the tide in our favor today.'

When night fell upon the battlefield, the firing gradually ceased and both sides spent most of the night in constructing such temporary defenses as lay in their power, using rails, logs, brush and what earth could be scooped up with out spade or shovel. The morning found us still confronting each other and ready to renew hostilities. There was more or less sharpshooting and reconnoitering in the morning. I had gotten with my command. That golden hearted, lovable gentleman, gallant Frank Jones of Thomas County, who was then adjutant, took me, as I had a good mount, with him on an uncomfortable reconnoitering ride and we came near being shot by Yankee sharpshooters. Poor dear comrade! He received his death wound later that same day when, after eating the last sorry meal with some of us, he laughingly said, 'Eat, drink and be merry, for to-morrow you may die.' As he stormed the works, leading the men, a piece of shell tore away his side, exposing the lungs and heart. Still he lived nearly two days in that condition. I held his hand when he died, after that last faint smile which I shall never forget. The nobility of his soul shined out as a glittering gem among the purest, gentlest, knightliest gentlemen whose wealth and blood were spent and poured out, a willing libation on the altar of Southern liberty.

Fitz Lee's command having been delayed by a misleading guide the day before, having fortunately intercepted a portion of Sheridan's force in charge of our captured men and horses (among which was the horse I rode that morning), now swung into position and in the afternoon the battle was on in earnest all along the line. Our men, leaping over their own rude breast-works, charged grandly forward, taking the enemy's works (after stubborn fighting, for Sheridan and his men were good fighters as well as runners) and driving him back and then procuring their horses, Hampton's forces pressed Sheridan far below Richmond, where a few days later the affairs of Nances and Haws Shops occurred.

The Trivilian battle field, as Gen. Jubal Early said of it in passing that way a few days afterwards, resembled a hard fought infantry battle. Our losses in Cobb Legion were heavy, but it was a glorious victory snatched from what at one time seemed almost defeat. Being disabled, I was about the field hospital for two or three days helping care for the wounded, near Mr. West's place in the Green Spring neighborhood and while I saw much of war and human suffering there, I also witnessed the devotion and heroism of those angels of mercy and loving kindness, the lovely women—mothers and daughters of that far famed Green Spring neighborhood—to our boys and our holy cause. Their sacrifice of themselves, their time and all they possessed was complete, lavishly and charmingly bestowed, while they wept because they had no more to give and could not do more to alleviate pain and suffering.

It is glory enough to have suffered all that fell to our lot and fought in defense of the noble women of the South. No Monument of chiselled stone or polished marble, however costly, can ever be erected which will adequately commemorate their fame and matchless devotion, but their memory is forever enshrined in the hearts of those who wore the gray.''

Confederate
Cavalry Bugle

G.   FIRST LIEUTENANT ALLEN EDENS

Commander, Co. E, Fourth South Carolina Cavalry
Butler's Brigade, Hampton's Division, ANVA

Below is an excerpt from a letter dated June 22, 1864, written at Bottoms Bridge, Virginia, by Lieutenant Allen Edens to his wife, Christian Chisholm Edens of Clio, South Carolina, following the Battle of Trevilian Station, Virginia, June 11-12, 1864.

> "Bottoms Bridge, Va.
> Chichomona River
> June 22, 1864

My Dear Chrisey—

I have had a time—we have been on the tramp for 15 days—have fought 2 hard battles and had several skirmishes—we left Mechanicsville on Tuesday morning the ninth of June and traveled two days and nights and attacked the enemy Sat. morning at sunrise near Trevilian Station and had a severe battle lasting all day without decision on either side—the battle was renewed on Sunday at 3 oclock and raged with great fury until dark when the Yanks gave way and fled like wild goats leaving the ground strewed with dead and dying—our loss was heavy but not half that of the enemy. Our company lost 1 killed, 1 severely wounded and 8 captured. Sunday we had 5 wounded making 15 for both days. Loss of the Regt. about 90. Our whole loss will not exceed 600—that of the Yanks 1,500 - 2,000. I fired all my cartridges away—had three men wounded in the same jam of the fence by the balls—we was exposed to a galling fire both from cannon and small arms but God was our help in trouble—one thing I know the Yankees was severely punished—

Allen"

H. (1)   PRIVATE EDWARD L. WELLS

Co. K, Fourth South Carolina Cavalry
(Charleston Light Dragoons)
Butler's Brigade, Hampton's Division, ANVA

From Edward L. Wells comes an outstanding eyewitness account of the Battle of Trevilian Station, Virginia. His perceptive review of the action is as follows:

"In the afternoon Mechanicsville was reached, and there the night was spent. This place, like all old camping-grounds, was well stocked with that insect which has a special fondness for lean soldiers, familiarly known in those days as 'I.F.W.' ('in for the war'). On first acquaintance he was sickening, and his memory is unsavory; so let us mention him no more. There was much interested discussion and speculation that evening as to where the command was about to move, for it was understood that it was to march early the next morning, and five days' rations had been issued. Certainly a raid, or expedition of some kind was intended, but neither officers nor men had the slightest idea of where they were going. Change is usually welcome, and the mystery added a charm to the expected movement. Some said they were going to Washington; others perhaps looked forward to dancing in Baltimore, but no one doubted that there would be, at all events, plenty of 'music' of a certain kind.

Early on the following morning the brigade was put on the march, proceeding north of Richmond. A steady walk was kept up all day, and when a halt for the night was ordered, some thirty miles had been made. The next morning the march was resumed. At about noon a short halt was made, and Gen. Butler then sent the Adjutant of the Fourth to say to one of the 'Dragoons,' whose horse had become slightly lame, that he was to quietly fall out of ranks, and return to the Reserve Camp near Mechanicsville, where unserviceable animals and men had been left. This incident was thought to indicate a long expedition, but at that time the Brigade Commander himself was not aware of his destination. It was not until the halt at night, about three miles from Trevilian Station, that he knew the object of the movement was to intercept Sheridan. This news soon became known among the men, and few of them will ever forget the occasion; the quiet summer evening, the cool crisp air, so grateful after the heat and well-nigh unendurable dust of the two days' march, and the blue mountain-ridges in the distance looking peaceful and pretty, and refreshing to the eyes.

There was that famous regiment, the 'Second,' corps d'elite of the 'Old Army.' It had been organized in 1855, with Albert Sidney Johnston as Colonel, afterwards the hero, whom many rank in ability the third among Confederate commanders, and whose death at Shiloh, after he had reduced Grant's army to a mass of fugitives, they think a calamity second only to that of Stonewall Jackson; the Lieutenant-Colonel had been Lee, 'A being apart and superior to all others in every way;—that towered far above all men on either side in that struggle;—the great American of the Nineteenth Century.'* Hardee, Van Dorn, Kirby Smith, Hood, Fields, Major, Fitz Hugh Lee, men of note on the Southern side, and Thomas, Johnson, Palmer and Stoneman on the Northern, had been officers in this regiment. Then there were the First and Fifth Regulars, and Custer's Brigade, and some New Jersey Regiments, which were rated high, and other crack bodies. The artillery had also been carefully selected, and was in excellent order, the batteries having recently been reduced from six to four guns each. There were six complete batteries, aggregating twenty-four** pieces, whilst the guns on the Confederate side numbered only twelve,*** or one to two of their adversaries.

Divining Sheridan's intentions, Hampton had succeeded in interposing his command on the night of June 10th, between the enemy and Gordonsville, thus covering that place and Charlottesville. During the night scouts brought in the intelligence that Sheridan had crossed the North Anna at Carpenter's Ford. He was entirely unaware that Hampton was in the neighborhood, and in quest of him, and had incautiously placed behind himself a river, supposing that he would have an undisputed march. He had 'reckoned without his host,' but so completely was he in the dark about Hampton's movements, that when his advance guard came into collision the next morning with the Confederate force, he mistook the latter for some local militia endeavoring to protect their homes.****

---

*Lord Wolseley, McMillan's Magazine, March, 1887.

**Information obtained from the Federal General J.M. Robertson, at that time stationed at White House, who was attending to business connected with the organization of batteries with four guns instead of six.

***Information obtained from Major Hart of Hart's Battery. The batteries were Hart's. Breathed's and Thomson's, of four guns each.

****Captain Manigault, Adjutant of the Fourth, who fell into the hands of the enemy in the early morning of June 11th, learned this fact from conversations with Federal officers. Also see General Torbert's Report.

Hampton at once realized the opportunity thus afforded him by his foe, and prepared to utilize it with his usual vigor. The moment had come not merely for checking his adversary, but for absolutely destroying him; surprised and driven back upon the river, his entire force would be devoted to ruin. The plan of the battle the writer believes was this:

In the morning at dawn Butler's and Young's Brigades of Hampton's Division would encounter the enemy advancing on the road leading from Clayton's Store (near the river) to Trevylian Station, on the (then styled) Virginia Central Railroad, whilst to the other brigade, Rosser's, was assigned the duty of covering a road on the left, branching from Clayton's Store, and leading towards Gordonsville. Fitz Hugh Lee's Division, camped that night near Louisa Court House, was ordered to move promptly to the attack down a road leading from that point to Clayton's Store, his left flank and Hampton's right thus mutually covering each other. This disposition was intended to place the two divisions united at Clayton's Store, Hampton driving the enemy in front, Fitz Hugh Lee flanking him on his left, and Rosser advancing to press his right flank, whilst the river blocked retreat. Then, it could be reasonably expected, would be dealt the coup-de-grace to Sheridan's host. The plan was simple, and admirable; why it was not completely successful will appear from the events to be related.

The air was chilly, the sweet-scented clover dripping with dew, and a bracing breeze coming from the dark mountain ridges, as the cavalrymen mounted in the first grey light of that June morning. A small piece of musty corn-bread hastily munched represented the only available substitute for breakfast, and some of the 'Dragoons' had not even that, their negroes left at camp having retained the major part of the rations for five days there issued. Happy then would have been that mythical personage, who, it is said, 'would rather fight than eat,' but he would have mustered very few disciples among all those fellows with empty stomachs. However, there was soon something else besides hunger to think of, for the programme was commenced by a mounted charge of a squadron from the Fourth, which brushed aside a Federal* picket from the road leading to Clayton's Store, and then the brigade was dismounted and deployed on both sides of the road. Advancing a little distance the enemy was encountered, and the firing became quite brisk. The 'Dragoons' (what was left of them, some twelve men,) went into action under the command of Lieutenant Cordes, who was assigned to that duty from one of the other companies of the regiment. He was a good officer, and much liked, but he was allowed scant time for enjoying the honor of leading the crack company of the Brigade, for he was soon wounded, and

---

*It appears to have been from the Second Regulars (Lee-Johnston Regiment formerly).

then the 'Dragoons' were in their normal condition again, without a commissioned officer. Lieut. Harleston, who, as has been said, had been detailed for temporary service in attending to ordnance at Richmond, had hastened to rejoin his company, but did not succeed in accomplishing this that morning.

Butler's and Young's Brigades were performing the part allotted to them on the centre of the line; the enemy was being pressed back. Here Thomas Lining was killed, and a better fellow never wore the 'Dragoons'' uniform. He was colourbearer of the Fourth, but, as already explained, it was not considered advisable to carry the flag in fighting on foot in a wooded country; during the actions at Hawes' Shop and Cold Harbor he had chafed very much at being compelled to remain with the horses, and he told the writer on the march to Trevylian, that he could not endure again such a position, and had arranged to carry a rifle and go with his old company into their next fight. So on this morning he had exchanged places with an ill man, taking his rifle and cartridge-box and falling-in with the 'Dragoons.' He was shot through the femoral artery, and died before assistance could be rendered. About this time also, Wells was disabled by a bullet.

Rosser, too, was carrying out his instructions, so that on the left, as well as centre, everything was progressing satisfactorily. Surprised, and stuck in an awkward situation, Sheridan was being hemmed in for destruction.

But suddenly the startling news came that the enemy in force was in the rear of the Confederate position, having passed around the right flank of Hampton's Division, which was not covered, as had been expected, by Fitz Hugh Lee's Division; the cause of this is unknown to the writer, but such was the fact. This, of course, changed the whole situation, and necessitated an instant alteration of the battle plan. There was no time for thinking either; action quick as lightning was required to save the Division from utter demolition. Rosser was therefore ordered by Hampton to dash from his position on the left, and charge the enemy then in the road behind the Confederate line of battle. This vigilant officer had already perceived that something was wrong; he had noticed an immense cloud of dust rising to the skies from the place where the horse-holders of Butler's Brigade had been left. He immediately put his command into a gallop, and promptly struck the enemy, Custer's Brigade. This later corps was occupying a road near the Railroad Track, and had captured some horses, a few wagons, and three caissons. It was here that Burgess Gordon of the 'Dragoons,' being a horseholder, fell into their hands. Rosser, with sabres and revolvers, made short work of Custer; taking from him his captures, besides making nearly an entire regiment prisoners, and driving most of the rest back as fugitives upon Fitz Hugh Lee, who, in consequence, bagged four caissons, and Custer's head-quarter wagon. It was necessary afterwards to read the papers found in the latter, in hopes of discovering some military information which might prove of value; in doing this, racy female correspondence came to light, but we will not 'tell tales out of school.'

As large numbers of dismounted cavalry had by this time pressed on to support Custer, it became necessary for the Confederates to move back in order to take up another line and form a junction with Fitz Lee. In carrying out this purpose Colonel Rutledge with the Fourth, was ordered to reverse the position of his regiment so as to check the enemy in their rear. It was then that Boone of the 'Dragoons' was killed, a fine athletic youth, bold as a lion, merry as a lark, always 'the life' of the camp; he died, no doubt, with a smile on his face, as a brave man should. Fairly, too, went down; he was acting as a courier that day, and lost his life while gallantly riding along the line in the face of a hot fire, carrying an order from the commanding officer. In fact, the hostile lines were at that moment so near together, that he must have known the chances were greatly against his coming back alive, but nevertheless he did his duty unflinchingly. Rutledge found the enemy in overwhelming numbers on the railroad, but managed by good judgment to keep his regiment interposed between the Federals and the rest of Butler's Brigade, until he succeeded, by moving some distance to his right, in taking position on the new line, which was successfully established near Trevylian Station by Hampton. Attempts were made by Sheridan to dislodge Hampton's Division from this place, but they were fruitless, both sides occupying their ground that night.

Sunday morning found the opposing forces holding the same relative positions, but by midday Fitz Lee had formed a junction with Hampton's Division, and was assigned a place from which he was to support the latter in case of an attack.

The brilliant military ability displayed by Hampton on Saturday, in extricating his command from a fearfully perilous situation, produced by no fault of his, should make this day memorable for all time. It was an occasion, too, on which his personal heroism, and the extraordinary influence exercised over his soldiers, marked him as the born warrior.

The position now occupied was, as has been stated, near Trevylian Station, on the (then styled), Virginia Central Railroad (now Chesapeake and Ohio Railroad), covering the wagon road and other approaches to Gordonsville. To carry out the purposes of his expedition, it was necessary for Sheridan to proceed in that direction, but Hampton's 'carriage stopped the way.'

Quiet reigned during that Sunday morning, but it was the silence attending earnest preparation for effort on one side, and resolute unyielding determination on the other. At about three o'clock in the afternoon, Colonel Rutledge of the Fourth, was sitting on the top of a pile of wood by the railroad track, when the crack of a sharp-shooter's rifle was heard in the distance, and after an interval a bullet struck one of the logs with a thud. Gen. Butler, standing near, remarked, 'That is the opening of the ball.' And so it was.

Butler's Brigade occupied the left of the line, and the General now ordered Col. Rutledge of the Fourth to proceed further in that direction, so as more effectually to hold the point where the main road crossed the railway through a broad cut in the embankment. Most of the Fifth and the Sixth Regiments were on the right of the Fourth, and were posted chiefly behind the railroad embankment, which served as a partial breastwork; but the Fourth had very little cover, except a rail fence along the wagon-road, before it reached the railroad crossing. The brigade line thus formed was not straight, the Fourth and a detachment from the Fifth on its left, holding the critical point at the cut in the embankment, and extending thence to the left along the road at an angle.

Sheridan 'meant business,' as he soon showed. His dismounted regiments charged with energy the positions held by Butler's Brigade and the Fourth Regiment, with the detachment from the Fifth, was so placed that these necessarily sustained the heaviest part of the onsets.

Yankee sharpshooters were stationed in the edge of the woods and in the Ogg house, until Hart's battery destroyed it. The Second squadron, under Captain Davis, faced the open field at the extreme end of which at least a thousand yards from us, we could see the Yankee cavalry form in line for charging. The bugles would sound the charge, but there was no horseback charge by the Yankees that day. They would prepare for the charge, when the fire from our long Enfield rifles would create such consternation, then they would come to a halt and disappear behind a body of woods, then reappear and try the process again and again, until they had made thirteen different unsuccessful attempts to make the charge. Meantime we were getting in our deadly work, while they were making good the old saying that 'he who hesitates is lost.' Prisoners captured the next day stated that our fire was so great at such a distance that it was thought we had been reinforced by infantry, and could not believe that only a brigade of South Carolina Cavalry was in their front. On the second day's fight, the Fifth cavalry lost in the day's fighting, 6 killed and 41 wounded. Sgt. R.M. Glaze of the Fifth Regiment had his head blown away by a cannon ball.

74

While this was in progress, Fitz Lee, by Hampton's orders, reinforced the left of Butler by Wickham's Brigade, which was posted behind the railroad embankment, and took the rest of his division, by a detour to the left to strike the Federals on their right flank. Six charges were made by the enemy, and all had been repulsed. After each, however, the foe had retired to a lesser distance, so that after his sixth unsuccessful attempt to carry the position, he was established at perilously close proximity to the Confederate line, some places only a few yards distant. Moreover, he had managed to put some sharp-shooters in a farmhouse, from the upper windows of which they were able to shoot down with considerable effect. Worse still, six guns had been brought into position and were partially enfilading the entire brigade line, but more completely the Fourth. These pieces were capitally served, and were doing severe execution, the shrapnell killing men lying down behind the rail-fence breast-work as if they were in an entirely open field, a very hard thing for any troops to endure steadily, without the prospect of relief. His artillery also silenced a Confederate battery supporting the line, and was indeed 'having it all its own way.' To add to the trying stature of the situation, ammunition had run short; it had been necessary to collect cartridges from the bodies of the dead and wounded, and now a very insufficient number remained with any of the regiments with which to resist further assaults, and the Fourth had nearly empty boxes.

There was a lull, almost a complete cessation in the firing, except on the part of the artillery; the enemy was 'girding up his loins' for another and a final charge. To each Federal private a dram of whiskey was served, and a plentiful supply of metallic shells for his breechloader.

All this while the Confederate troopers were enduring the trying ordeal with patient resolution. One young officer, as unmindful of his own danger as if his skin were bullet-proof, was walking down the line of his company encouraging the men, who were lying behind what cover there was, to for-titude. He reminded them of mothers and wives, sisters and sweethearts, who at their homes in the 'far South,'; in their venerable much loved churches, were at that very moment sending up to the Most High prayers for their safe-ty. It was an effective form of eloquence, for he was a sincere and brave man. Others again arrived at an equally desirable mental condition for fighting, in saying, or thinking, 'Let the beggars come on, and be damned!' It amounted to the same thing in the end, for all, saints and sinners, were ready to 'face the music.' It was promised you that the Cavalry under Hampton should in-augurate a style of fighting equal in stubborn tenacity, as well as dash, to that of the magnificent infantry of the Army of Northern Virginia; then and there was the promise fulfilled; then and there was the pledge kept before the face of God and man.

It was at this time that Major Hart, who was working his guns on the right of the line, received through Captain Jeffords an urgent message from Gen. Butler, requesting him to bring his battery as quickly as possible, to where the Fourth and Fifth were stationed. Hart took two of his guns, all that could be spared, and galloped to the point indicated. He found the Federal sharp-shooters in the farm-house were doing great damage, and to them he paid his first attentions. Dividing his detachments and thus manning two of the abandoned guns already mentioned, he concentrated the fire of these and his own with short-range fuses upon the house, and in less than one minute from the time the first piece opened, he had the building in flames, and the sharp-shooters scurrying out for their lives. Then turning to the Federal battery on the right of the house, he poured into it so rapid and accurate a fire, that it was driven away in between ten and fifteen minutes. The importance of this service, thus gallantly, promptly and efficiently performed, can readily be appreciated, and every one connected with the cavalry well knows that on this and many a similar critical occasion Major Hart proved himself indeed 'the man for Galway.'

At nearly the same moment at which Major Hart reached the ground, as related, the sorely needed ammunition also arrived. The wagon came rattling down the road with the mules on a full run, the driver lashing and cracking his whip. He continued at the same furious pace along the line in plain view of the enemy, a man in the rear of the wagon throwing out the packages, which are instantly caught-up, and the contents quickly found their way into the hungry cartridge-boxes. It was well done for a wagoner, and now 'Richard was himself again.'

At this hour the setting sun was just above the mountain-ramparts with which nature has guarded 'the Valley,' lighting up the peaks with a blaze of glory, touching the lower ridges with the soft dreamy colours of hope, the nearer foot-hills looking almost despairingly black by contrast. It is strange how sights like this, witnessed at important moments in man's life, will linger always in the memory. Before the sun should sink behind the fair warders of 'the Valley,' was to be decided the fate of Gordonsville, Charlottesville and Lynchburg, perhaps of Richmond.

The enemy advanced in force 'to finish up the job,' to push the Confederates out of their position by sheer weight of numbers. They concentrated on Butler's Brigade, special gatekeeper of the road they wished to traverse, and the Fourth and part of the Fifth, as holding the key, were markedly singled out for attentions. One body marched straight for the cut in the embankment; it moved with beautiful precision, in close order, shoulder to shoulder, the rifles, Spencers or Winchesters, held horizontally at the hip, and shooting continuously. On they came, and a few steps in advance, on one side, strode the leader, a large fine-looking man, apparently a gentleman, with topboots extending above his knees, and corduroy riding-trousers. His right arm was bent holding his cocked revolver pointing perpendicularly upwards at the 'Ready!' and he counted time to keep his troopers in regular step. He presented a fine mark, but somehow no bullets, it seemed, could hit him, and when any of his men dropped, the rest closed up beautifully and marched straight on. It was a handsome sight, always to be remembered, but not an agreeable one just at that moment. This brave fellow had almost reached the rail breast-work, when suddenly he stopped; very slowly the right arm descended until the pistol grasped in the hand pointed to the earth; he made an effort as if striving to brace-up, and then all at once the legs gave way, and it collapsed upon the ground, an inert lifeless thing. Immediately his men broke and ran. Just at that moment one of Hart's shells exploded an ammunition wagon, or a limberchest, which evidently threw the enemy into some confusion. At that, as if by an electric impulse common to them all, the whole Confederate line leaped to their feet, sprang over the temporary breast-work with an exultant yell, and charged. The foe was driven back in disorder pell-mell upon his reserves, and at the same time Fitz Lee was seen pushing steadily forward in an open space, doubling-up their right flank. Then the great big fiery-faced Sun, having staid so long to see the fight over, sank joyously from sight behind the black mountains, for the day was won; Hampton had by sheer skill and pluck wrenched victory from the bloody fangs which had well-nigh rent his vitals.

After that it was only a question with Sheridan how to get away, and with Hampton how to prevent him. Butler's Brigade continued to occupy their former line, and the enemy kept up an irregular skirmish to cover their retreat, but it amounted to little more than an affair of sharp-shooters, and by ten o'clock all was quiet on that part of the field. It was before the last charge was repulsed that Col. Rutledge of the Fourth, while standing at the outside of his regimental line, had the shoulder and upper part of the sleeve of his coat cut by a bullet. Supposing the incident to be caused by some accidental shot, he thought nothing of it, but shortly afterwards the breast of his coat was furrowed by another ball. This was also attributed to chance, but just then one of the officers of the regiment came up to speak to him, and had hardly commenced doing so when his cheek was scratched by a bullet, and soon afterwards another ploughed through his beard, tearing out a handful of hair. All these shots came from the same quarter, and it was therefore concluded were fired with 'malice pretense.' Naturally people cannot be expected to like having their clothes torn, faces scratched, and beards plucked so unceremoniously; so two men apt at exhortation were quietly sent forward to find this rude fellow, and protest against such conduct. These crawled along cautiously in the proper direction, and were not long in espying their man; he was a big red-haired Celt, occupying a slight elevation on which was a tree, from behind which he was peering out with cocked rifle watching for another pot-shot, as if engaged in land-lord shooting. The two soldiers from the Fourth promptly served their protest, doing this simultaneously so as to leave an agreeable doubt as to which gave the settler, and down he sank all in a heap. The next morning they found this red-haired person of homicidal proclivities stiff and stark, with rifle full-cocked lying between his legs. 'They who take the sword, shall perish by the sword,' it is said, and we may suppose the same thing fairly applies to rifles.

The enemy availed himself of the darkness, and all that night was engaged in making good his escape. One of the 'Dragoons,' who had been wounded on Saturday morning and had been left at a farm-house, fell into the hands of the Federals during the evolutions preparatory to establishing the second Confederate line. This house was turned into a field-hospital by Sheridan's surgeons, and over the entire yard and some ground outside were lying the wounded and dying, with plenty of amputated legs and arms to match. The wounded prisoners were treated with humanity, but of course suffered much; however, roasting in the sun all day, and shivering with chattering teeth in a shower of rain on Saturday night, were compensated for by the tramping of thousands of hoofs on the road close by, as the enemy hurried past all Sunday night in full retreat, leaving behind their wounded in charge of one of their surgeons. It was at this field-hospital during Saturday and Sunday, that the 'Dragoon' mentioned received many kindnesses from a Sergeant and Private of the celebrated 'Second.' Both of these spoke in the warmest terms of respectful regard of Albert Sidney Johnston, and to this feeling for him was probably due in a great measure their good nature towards the wounded Confederate. It was a rather singular coincidence, that this same 'Dragoon,' happening in the early part of 1862 to be at one of the Forts in New York Harbor, heard there a sergeant, a big stalwart fellow, say excitedly to a knot of his comrades, 'I tell you Albert Sidney Johnston was the best man that ever walked on God's earth!'

The Dragoons had lost at Trevylian three killed; the officer assigned to command them and one man were wounded, and one (a horse-holder) was captured: a loss of fifty per cent. The Fourth Regiment suffered severely, but to what numerical extent the writer does not know, as Adjutant Manigault fell into the hands of the enemy in carrying a message on Saturday morning, when the opposing lines were only a few yards apart.

The Yankees displayed pluck and splendid courage that day in their attempt to drive us away, but were sadly in lack of a good cavalry leader. Sheridan was no match for Butler. He said a few days after his fight that that d—d man (meaning Butler) had given him more trouble with his South Carolina brigade than all the rebel cavalry put together. 'Praise, indeed, from Sir Hubert.'

The Fourth South Carolina Cavalry, under the gallant Colonel B.H. Rutledge, behaved most gallantly. Our losses in killed was fearful. I witnessed a most tragic and pathetic scene in the 'Bloody Angle.' While the Yankee battery was enfilading a part of our line along the railroad embankment, a shell knocked all the flesh off the right thigh of John Moss, leaving the thigh bone perfectly bare, even of blood, and in some mysterious way did not break it. When his brother Mat saw it, he at once ran to him, put his arms around him, when a Yankee sharpshooter shot him through the heart. He died lying across John's breast, who did not die for some little time afterwards. Both of these splendid soldiers—splendid in physique and splendid in courage—belonged to Company B, of the Sixth South Carolina Cavalry. This regiment was the greatest sufferer owing to the position it occupied in the 'Angle.' Either of the others, Fourth and Fifth, would have made the same record under the same circumstances. General Butler, Captain Jas. N. Lipscomb, his adjutant-general; his gallant young aide-de-camp, Nat. Butler; Major Chew, and several couriers, were the only mounted men on the line of our brigade, and I have looked back with wonder and amazement how it was they escaped in that deadly fire of the enemy. But such things 'are past finding out.' The men and horses of our division were so fatigued and jaded (the men having been without a morsel to eat from Friday until Monday afternoon, and the horses having been grazed only for an hour or two each night) we could not pursue Sheridan as vigorously as we desired. Sheridan's retreat was so precipitate that he could not wait for horses that showed signs of fatigue, but had them shot at once, and Colonel Zimmerman Davis counted over two thousand dead horses, with bullet holes in their heads, in the one hundred miles (averaging over twenty to the mile) from Trevilian to the White House on the Pamunky.

The total loss in Hampton's Division amounted to 612,* of which 295 were missing; that in Fitz Lee's was very light. I have no knowledge of a regular official report of his casualties in the battle of Trevylian having been made by Sheridan, but he states that he thinks those of his corps from May 4th to July 30th, aggregated 'between 5,000 and 6,000.' A large percentage of this punishment was inflicted at Trevylian, 977* prisoners (including 125

---

*Official Report of General Hampton.

wounded) having been taken from him in that battle, and during his retreat to the cover of the gunboats, and his killed and wounded were certainly correspondingly heavy.

On Monday Hampton pressed on in pursuit of the foe, who, having 'head-start,' succeeded in crossing the North Anna at Carpenter's Ford. As Sheridan was provided with a pontoon-train, which enabled him to cross rivers at any point, and as the Confederate force had none, it was necessary for the latter to remain on the Southern sides of the streams, so as to keep between him and Grant's army, and thus prevent the junction, which he was trying to effect. For several days the hostile columns thus marched on parallel lines, the enemy carefully avoiding a collision, until at length he reached the much-desired haven, the shelter of the gunboats at White House, on the Pamunkey River, after a skirmish there in which he was worsted. At this point he crossed during the night, and was met by reinforcements, in connection with which he moved down the river, and thence made for the Chickahominy, over which he passed at the Forge Bridges. At Nance's Shop on June 24th (or Samaria Church, as the fight is sometimes styled), he was struck by Hampton; his line was charged by the dismounted men, who handsomely carried the breast-works, and routed his command, which was charged and pursued by two mounted regiments. It was not until ten o'clock at night, and within two and a half miles of Charles City Court House, that he was able by speed of foot to shake off his pursuers, leaving behind, besides dead and wounded, 157* prisoners. From this place ʌe continued his retreat to Wyanoke Neck, and crossed the James River protected by his gunboats. Thus ended what is known as the 'Trevylian Campaign,' in which Sheridan was completely frustrated in the objects of his expedition, and driven by a force greatly inferior in numbers and materiel to his own, back to the cover of Grant's army. But if it had not been that on Saturday morning, June 11th, the right flank was uncovered—however, let us have done with 'buts.'

Gen. Hampton says 'the men could not have behaved better than they did' under 'their hard marches, their want of supplies, their numerous privations.'** And it was not long afterwards that General Butler obtained the well-won stars of a Major-General.

Gen. Custer's report of the Trevylian campaign is interesting, one might almost say edifying. Usually his style in official reports is somewhat florid, suggestive of an imagination not unlike Rider Haggard's, such expressions as 'driving the enemy,' 'routing them,' 'pursuit,' &c., being of frequent

---

*General Gregg, commanding Second Division, admits being driven, and losing 267 men.
**Official Report of General Hampton.

occurrence. His account of the operations of June 11th, however, is a little toned-down from the customary manner, and what he says of June 12th is in a diction of chastened sobriety. From General Merritt's report it is learned that the force which Butler's Brigade first encountered in opening the fight on June 11th, was the celebrated 'Second,' and that the Senior Captain in command was wounded at an early hour that morning. Gen. Torbert, commanding First Division, reports that on the night of June 10th, just before going into camp, the head of his column was attacked by ten or twelve men, which was the first time any Confederates had been seen during the expedition. These were in fact Hampton's scouts. He also says that the next morning he could obtain no definite news of any enemy, until encountering their pickets. This information accords with that received from other sources, proving that Sheridan was completely surprised at Trevylian. Torbert wanders, however, into the region of romance, when he remarks that on June 12th the Confederate force was 'reinforced by one or two regiments of infantry from Gordonsville.' The reason given by him for the retreat that night is, that they had as many of their men wounded as they 'could well take care of.' Later on, in summing up the campaign to July, he observes, 'When dismounted they (Confederates) have had a great advantage of us, from the fact that they have a very large Brigade of Mounted Infantry, armed with the rifled musket.' To one with 'a judicial mind' (as the newspapers say) it seems rather cool to call it an advantage to have muzzle-loaders against breech-loaders, but the remark is certainly a great compliment to the 'long-shooters,' and is an evidence of what a bete noire Butler's Brigade proved to those good people.

The impression derived from an examination of these portions of the reports of Sheridan's officers, which relate to the battle of Trevylian, cannot, I think, be otherwise than very unfavorable to the military reputation of that General. It is not necessary to 'read between the lines' to find evidence of want of caution, resulting in the surprise of his force, and of lack of proper knowledge of the topography of the country, so that after crossing the river his Brigade Commanders were almost groping in the dark in their intended advance. It is clear that Custer arrived in the rear of Hampton's Division, not in the pursuance of any definite plan, but that he simply wandered into that position through the gap in the Confederate line on Fitz Lee's left. When, however, Custer by a fortunate accident found himself there, he tried to press his advantage, and it was then that Sheridan should have concentrated overwhelmingly on Hampton's Division, and destroyed it, while without support. But he failed to utilize the golden moments, showing himself unable to cope with the vigor of his antagonist. He consumed the remainder of Saturday in a series of isolated and spasmodic attacks, in which his troops were ably handled as far as tactics were concerned, and fought hard, but in a blind fashion, apparently without any strategical plan. The next day he must have taken a late Sunday morning nap, for it was not until the afternoon that he attacked, and in the meantime Fitz Lee was allowed ample opportunity to make a long detour, which was throughout plainly traceable by the dust-clouds, and thus reunite his command with that of Hampton.

The experience of an officer of the Fourth, who was taken prisoner at Trevylian, will serve to illustrate the precipitancy of Sheridan's retreat. His rear guard began the march before daylight, and at first some confusion was observable, due doubtless to the supposed proximity of those villainous 'long-shooters.' After a little while, however, there were no more signs of disorder, and during the remainder of the march good discipline was manifest. This must be attributed in great measure to the large leaven of regulars in the mass, whose technical training and habits of routine would be especially valuable at such a time. The organization of the 'Old Army' was perhaps the most valuable asset of the dissolved Firm appropriated by the Northern Partners; an asset to which, by some legerdemain of reasoning, they became self-convinced they had of right an exclusive claim, merely because the manufactory, founded and maintained at the common expense, happened to be located at West Point. The prisoners were compelled to walk hard to keep pace with the rearguard, and as cavalrymen are at best but poor entries for a foot-race, it became necessary either to leave behind many on the road-side temporarily exhausted, or to give them occasional rests by dismounting regiments and putting Confederates in their saddles. The latter course was adopted, not at all from motives of humanity, but to prevent the loss of able-bodied prisoners, who, becoming in his keeping living skeletons, or ghastly corpses, it mattered not which to Secretary Stanton, represented so many rifles wrested from the slender line of gray encircling, with hearts and hands, the Southern Cross. The march on the second day of the retreat (Tuesday) was particularly hurried and distressing. One evening the Confederate officers had been halted near a commodious, spacious house on a large wheat plantation. It was a pretty home-like scene, that quiet residence surrounded by a rolling country with waving fields of 'golden grain' and sweet flowering clover, and soft blue mountains in the far distance; by contrast with their condition, it seemed to the jaded, half-dead prisoners that they were

'Full in the sight of Paradise,
Beholding Heaven and feeling Hell!'

82

Just then a brisk little man came out of a small tent pitched near the house, and, walking up to the group, saluted them civilly in semi-military fashion, and said: 'Gentlemen, I am sorry to have been obliged to march you so hard, but it is unavoidable. I have given orders that all the mattresses and bedding in this house shall be spread on the floors of the rooms, so as to accommodate as many of you as possible, for you will require all the rest you can get to enable you to stand the march to-morrow.' The speaker was 'Phil Sheridan.' On entering the building the Confederates were met by the lady of the house, who apologized for having no food with which to give them a meal. 'They have taken every morsel on the place, even my little children's supper,' said she. This had been done, not in the spirit of wanton destruction, but because the Federal troops pursued by Hampton were without rations, except some hard-tack, coffee and sugar, which still remained in their wagons, and were so closely pressed as to be unable to forage on the country in a regular manner.

By the casualties of battle, and by illnesses contracted in the service, the number of the Dragoons was now reduced to a very small fraction of the aggregate on their muster-roll when they marched for Virginia.''

H. (2) KING McLAURIN'S FIGHTING ANCESTORS
AT THE BATTLE OF TREVILIAN STATION, VIRGINIA

The newspaper article below reflects an unusual story of King McLaurin of St. Petersburg, Florida, whose paternal and maternal great-great grandfathers and three great-great uncles were in Co. E, Fourth South Carolina Cavalry. His maternal great-great grandfather was First Lieutenant Allen Edens, who commanded the unit. His great-great uncles were Lauchlin A., James W., and Loch B. McLaurin—the fighting Scots.

Floridian Visits Battlefield

King McLaurin and Colonel Walbrook D. Swank

A recent guest at Prospect Hill was King McLaurin, a business executive of St. Petersburg, Florida. Having read the book *The War and Louisa County 1861-1865* by Col. Walbrook D. Swank of Frederick Hall, McLaurin wanted to visit the site of the Battle of Trevilians where five of his ancestors fought with the Fourth South Carolina Cavalry of Gen. Matthew Butler's Brigade.

In the above picture Colonel Swank, a friend of McLaurin, points to shell holes in one of the chimneys of the Ogg house which was in the center of most of the action in the second day's fighting. The house was used as a hospital when the firing ceased.

A tragic and pathetic event occurred at the "Bloody Angle". A Yankee battery was enfilading a part of the Rebel line along the railroad embankment, a shell knocked all the flesh off the right thigh of John Moss, leaving the thigh bone perfectly bare, and in some mysterious way did not break it. When his brother Matt saw it, he at once ran to him and put his arms around him, when a Yankee sharpshooter shot him through the heart. He died lying across John's breast, who did not die for some little time afterwards. These men were members of Co. B, 6th South Carolina Cavalry which was fighting alongside the 4th South Carolina Cavalry.

I. THE BLOODY ANGLE

The Confederate Battle Flag flies at the "Bloody Angle", the crucial point in the Confederate battle line where Union troopers were repelled and defeated after numerous charges. There was a rail fence along the wagon road, before it reached the railroad crossing. Yankee sharpshooters were in the edge of the woods and in the Ogg house, seen in the left background of the picture, and did great damage until they were routed by the fire from Hart's artillery battery. The Ogg house became a field hospital after the firing ceased.

It was at the railroad embankment that a Yankee shell mortally wounded John Moss of Co. B., Sixth South Carolina Cavalry. As his brother Mat went to hold him in his arms, Mat was shot through the heart by a Yankee bullet. It was here too, that Sergeant R.M. Glaze of the Fifth South Carolina Cavalry had his head blown away by a Union cannon ball.

85

J. THE CADET COMPANY
SIXTH SOUTH CAROLINA CAVALRY

Butler's Brigade, Hampton's Division, ANVA

The story of the charge of "The Cadet Company" and its engagement at Louisa Court House and in the Battle of Trevilian Station, Virginia, is presented here by Lieutenant Alfred Aldrich, who participated in the fighting. The Cadet Company was made up of Cadets of The Military College of South Carolina, Charleston, South Carolina.

Court House, Louisa County, Virginia

Several hundred yards in front and northwest of the Court House on June 11, 1864, General Wade Hampton led the boys of "The Cadet Company" in a charge through a railroad excavation that repelled Union cavalry that was attacking Hart's artillery battery.

"Our first service with the Army of Northern Virginia was with the column of cavalry under Lieut. General Hampton, who went in pursuit of Sheridan when he made his last raid into the Valley.

The Confederates overhauled Sheridan at Louisa Court House, on June 11, 1864, and there was a sharp fight between the head of our column and the rear of the enemy's.

The Cadet Company had position near the front. During the fight, Hart's Battery was charged by a column of enemy cavalry when our line was in confusion passing through a railroad excavation. General Hampton dashed up to the right of the Sixth Cavalry to get a force to follow him in a charge to save the battery, and although the confusion was as great at this part of the line as elsewhere, thanks to the Citadel training, Lieutenants Nettles and Aldrich got their company aligned within a few seconds, and Gen. Hampton charged in line of battle with the Cadet Company, staying the enemy's onset until Gen. Rosser struck his flank, charging at the head of his own brigade.

The secret of success in battle, according to the great cavalry leader of the Western Army, Gen. N.B. Forrest, was 'to get there first with the most men.' Here was a critical moment when the day would have been lost, perhaps, if our great leader had not determined to 'get there first' with a handful of boys!

The day succeeding the fight at Louisa Court House, the battle of Trevilians, the most sanguinary cavalry engagement of the war, was fought.

The Cadet Company of the Sixth was in the battle when the firing began and in the last attack of the Federals when they were repulsed.

After the battle, the enemy's dead were thicker in front of that part of the line held by the Cadet than anywhere else.

Captain Humphrey was wounded in the leg, Lieut. Aldrich in the right thigh, left arm, and right shoulder; Sergeant Simms had a finger of his left hand shot off; Corporal Hodges was shot in the breast, and privates Gladney, Quattlebaum, and Hodge were wounded in the right leg, right side, and left arm respectively. There were other casualties in the recruited portion of the company.''

K. A SOUTH CAROLINIAN'S DEATH

Private Francis M. Moorer
Co. A, Fifth South Carolina Cavalry
Butler's Brigade, Hampton's Division, ANVA

Robert B. Wilkinson, Jr., of St. Matthews, South Carolina, purchased a copy of the author's book "The War and Louisa County, 1861-1865" and having read the account of the Battle of Trevilian Station, Virginia, he wrote the writer a letter about his ancestor being mortally wounded duing the engagement. His name was Private Francis M. Moorer of Co. A, Fifth South Carolina Cavalry, Butler's Brigade, Hampton's Division, Cavalry Corps, Army of Northern Virginia.

The following is an excerpt from the letter dated August 14, 1986:

"I'm sending you a brief description of my ancestor and his friend. If my memory is correct Beckwith was wounded by a shell fragment but I don't know how my ancestor was wounded.

I also want to thank you and your SCV camp and the residents of Louisa County for working to preserve the memory of the battle at Trevilian's. I would be most thankful for any new information you might uncover about this battle or artifacts connected with the 5th SC Cavalry. I have no idea what my ancestor's uniform might look like or what their flag looked like, but I do know they were probably armed with Enfield rifles. So any details will be appreciated. I'm presently searching for pictures of any of the 5th Cavalry.

As I told you, I'm going to research having a small memorial marker made to place somewhere near the battle site. I'm sure you will know the most appropriate area for this. I may be able to come up to bring the marker, it may be spring before I can.

Francis Marion Moorer and Lawrence Ransom Beckwith
at the Battle of Trevilian's Station

Francis Marion Moorer was the great-great-great uncle of Robert B. Wilkinson, Jr., and Captain John L. Wilkinson, USAF, of the Wade Hampton Camp #273 of Columbia, S.C. He was born Jan. 1, 1825, in Orangeburgh District, being named for the 'Swamp Fox,' (Francis Marion, who was one of South Carolina's heroes of the first war for independence) under whom his grandfather served in 1781 as a lieutenant. At the time of his enlistment on Dec. 21, 1861, 'Frank' as he was known, was a moderately successful planter. His plantation 'Magnolia Grove,' was built in 1810 and inherited from his father. It was built adjacent to his great grandfather's land (who was one of the first settlers of Orangeburg, S.C., in 1735, a Swiss). He was enlisted at the age of 36, in the 20th Regiment, S.C. Volunteer Infantry, later Company B, under Capt. P.A. McMichael, serving on Sullivan's Island and the defenses of Charleston, S.C. On Feb. 1, 1863, he requested transfer to the 5th S.C. Cavalry, Company A and served with them in Charleston until called to Virginia. While serving under General Wade Hampton's command, he was mortally wounded in the fighting at Trevilian's Station, Va., on June 11, 1864. He died the next morning. His younger friend, Sgt. Lawrence Ransom Beckwith, marked his grave. (Beckwith was also wounded in that battle.) Beckwith who was to become Frank's nephew after the war, either during the recovery from his wound or after the war, returned to the grave with Frank's brother, John Lewis Moorer and a two horse wagon. They recovered his remains in some sort of bag and solemnly rode the 460 miles back to their home. His final resting place was the old family burying ground on his great grandfather's land. Frank's widow and two daughters survived the barbaric horde of Gen. William T. Sherman eight months after his death but only one daughter was to survive past 1880 on the impoverished plantation.''

Private
Francis Marion Moorer

Sergeant
Lawrence Ransom Beckwith

Certificate Recommending Extension of Furlough

Sergeant L. F. Beckwith of Co. B. 10 S.C. Cav. Regt.
Butler Brigade. (Post Office Coin, S.C.)

having been granted a furlough on the 5. Jany. "1864.
at Charlotte, N.C. by Maj. Ex Board

and having appeared before this Board for recommendation for extension of furlough, we do hereby
certify that we have carefully examined him and find that he is convalescent from Shell Wound
in left wrist, received 11 June 1864 in Battle at Sheridans Station

And in consequence thereof, he will not, in our opinion, be fit for duty in a less period than Thirty
days, for which time we recommend an extension of his, furlough, under General Order No. 141, Par.
V., Adjutant and Inspector-General's Office, October 29, 1863.

_____ Surgeon, P. A. C. S.

EXAMINING BOARD. _____ Surgeon, P. A. C. S. BOARD

J. M. Miller _____ Surgeon, P. A. C. S.

Columbia, S.C.
2 September 1864.

[DUPLICATE.]

91

L. PRIVATE ISAAC S. CURTIS

Co. A, Ninth Virginia Cavalry
Beale's Brigade, W.H.F. Lee's Division, ANVA

Copies of letters by Isaac S. Curtis, written at Sherman, Texas, September 4, 1911, and March 27, 1912, to Alex F. Rose, a former comrade-in-arms, are printed below. Curtis was a member of Company A, Ninth Virginia Cavalry and carried messages to General Wade Hampton at the Battle of Trevilian Station.

"Sherman Texas
September the 4th 1911

Sheridans Raid but thwarted in his plans
by Gen'l Wade Hampton.

On about the 12th of June Genl Grant planned to deceive Genl Lee by mkaing a faint with a portion of his Cevalry by giving fight near Hanover C.H., at the same time Sheridan with three of his best Brigades to counter charge back north up the North Anna River, believing Grant with his infantry would soon engage Genl Lee by making his flank movement south of Hanover C.H. that Genl Lee would be so absorbed that he, Sheridan, would make a complete circuit around Lee's rear going up the North Anna and move west by way of Louisa C.H. crossing the James River up near Linchburg and return up apparent on the west side of the Appomatox River near Stevensberg and meet Wilson who was at the time on a raid up from the West side, I was instructed to learn as quickly as possible the movement of Sheridan with his three Brigades. I left Hanover alone at night and went up the North Anna near Beaverdam Station there crossed the North Anna, and about 9 o'clock that night I found the column move forth I soon captured two soldiers and they knew nothing more then they had six days rations. I at once sent my companion Zack Scott back with a note to Genl Hampton telling him my idea was that Sheridan was making a raid to out all our Armys, cummunication north and return to the Army west of Petersburg this was correct. The next morning I again communicated with Genl Hampton however during this time Hampton was marching north parallel with Sheridan on the East of the River and Hampton on the West Sheridan after getting high up and nearly opposite Louisa C.H. turned west to Travillion Station.

Sheridan on reaching Travillion Station found Hampton in his front with Wickums Brigade also Rosser and Burgess Brigades and Butler that morning I was at Mansfields getting something to eat it was considerable up in the day, while their many Yankey Cavelry come they too was after something to eat, I made it convenient to get away as soon as possible which I did, I made for our Cavelry which at that time was engaging the enemy in my hearing, I fortunately reached our line where Genl Wickams Brigade was and I at once asked the whereabouts of Genl Hampton I was directed and had a mango with me to Genl. Hampton. I found the Genl sitting on his horse at Louisa C.H. I soon made know the conditions of thing in his front I told him the Brigades of Sheridans command consisted of Custer, Beauford & Greggs, and he Hampton at once had Rosser & Butler to strike them on the Flank. In a few hours he had Sheridan counter marching returning at almost the same route he came, I followed them sometimes was with them until we got back to York Town. I had some of the most interesting episodes on this trip I ever had in all my life things occured that will never be forgotten,

Yours truly
I S Curtis''

"Dear Comrade (Alex F. Rose)

Zack Scott wrote this up one at Galveston but he died and I do not know what become of it. This is one of the best things I ever did I was with Yankey every night, I had some fun with them when I got back down about Bowling Green I crossed the York River near the White House You can read and correct this and if you wish you can publish it.

Your friend Isaac
(S. Curtis, 9th Va., Cav.)"

Sherman, Texas
3/27/12

Mr A F Rose
My Friend & Comrade

I am enclosing you a piece I have written. I left out many things too bad to be made known to the public. You have heard me tell it. I killed a member of the 18th New York who was trying to rape a lady near White Chimneys in New Kent County and many other such acts. Doctor Jim Coleman and myself run on to five fellows near Guinea Station that had been to his Mothers and robbed them of all valuables cut open the Feather Beds and mistreated them, you know we paid them back for their conduct. Please look over this and if you think it woth publishing or should be published you can do so I do not like to blow my own horn in such cases.

We are simply downed out in this country at this time, rain, rain all the time has been very cold but now more pleasant. when your letter come I was at the Hot Wells I have had the Exema terrible hope to get over it. It has been some better for the last few days. It has cost me lots money for the last two months and lots annoyance.

I will be glad to hear from you. Say I wrote a piece Headed what is a Confederate Sodier and what does he stand for, it was published in the Ft. Worth Record there has been many comments on it,

With Regards to yourself and Wife
Your Friend & Comrade
I S Curtis"

"Sherman, Texas

(Continuous and Dangerous Service for Two Weeks)

March 27th 1912

About the 10th of June 1864 Genl U S Grant with his immense Army had been engaged in Battle with Genl R E Lee's raggad and half starved Army around Spotsylvania C. House for about a week Genl Grants immense Army being greatly in excess of nombers to that of Genl. Lee's moved by the left flank to the North Anna River. Genl Lee, engaged him at Cold Harber and forced Genl Grant to abandon his idea of going into Richmond, Genl Sheridan had the largest Corp, Cavelry that was ever organized during the Civil War. on the 10th June he made a faint demonstration at Hanover C.H. at the same time he was countermarching. Three Brigades Cavelry, and moving in the direction of Gordensville, on the East side of the North Anna River Genl Lee anticipated this movement and I was one of the Scouts sent to get such information; as I could and report same to Genl Wade Hampton who was in readiness to move North, on the West Side of the North Anna River. I lost no time in crossing the North Anna River at Beaver Dam Bridge and in a very short time we, Zack Scott and myself, was out on the road with Sheridens command, we captured two of them more for information then booty, they only knew they had 6 days rations was all. I sent Scott out to Genl Hampton at once telling him my idea was that Sheridan would make a raid around Lee's Army and return to Genl Grant at Petersberg, I did not report to Genl Hampton any more untill I got with the Enemy at a Mr. Mansfield near Louisa C.H. Genl Fitz Lee was at that time fighting Beufords Bragade near a cut in the R.R. when I got into our lines, Genl Fitz Lee, sent a man with me to Genl Hampton who was at the Court House. I found him sitting on his Horse in the street and give him the information that led to the attack on the left flank of Sheridens command. In three or four hours he had Sheriden on the retreat. I returned with Sheriden and did not rejoin Genl Hampton untill Sheriden got to York Town and there found Genl Hampton ready to meet him. Then come the fight at Haws Shop as warm day as I ever felt. Water was very scarce and the men suffered very much both for water and something to eat, it was this day that Captain Jams Pollard lost his leg or was badly wounded in the foot. I left Genl Hampton after this and over took our Infantry at Petersberg. The next morning the 27th of June the Enemy broke our lines at a House in a grove on the Weldon Petersberg R.R. Finegans Fla. Brigade was repulsed and Genl Mahone was ordered to retake the brokin line which he did but the Enemy had a very strong line in support of the first line therefore could not hold the works. I was instructed to investigate conditions and report by day the next morning, this was one of the hazardous undertakings I ever had knowing when the Armys were in engaged it was very difficult to get into the lines. I went to a Mr Reaves near Ream Station and while there three Federal Toopers rode up and they saw me eating June Apples that I had gotten out Mr Reaves orchard and they got a supply of Apples themselves and confiscated a chicken or so and left for there camp. It was then my oppotunity to go with them which I did. I went to The Tavern near this place, then to a Tobacco House where Genl Bursides had his Hd Qts and found the enemy had been reinforced by a portion of Sedgwick Corp. I made my way out by the same route I had entered the lines but on nearing our Pickets as I thought I met a squad of Federal Cavelry and I was compelled to abandon my horse and take to brush which enabled us to make my escape and was take in charge by the 1st North Carolina Cavelry and sent out to Genl Lee's Hd Qts near Petersberg. after my report there was no further effort made to retake the lost portion of the line, I went there that evening to Stoney Creek and reported to Genl Chamblisss who had intercepted Genl Wilson who was trying to get back to the Army. Genl Chambliss had his Brigade and fought the Wilson Raiders all night and the next morning they began to retreat.

Yours Truly
I S Curtis''

M. PRIVATE WILLIAM AUGUSTUS LAW

Co. I, Sixth South Carolina Cavalry
Butler's Brigade, Hampton's Division, ANVA

The following is a story of the war and Battle of Trevilian Station, as told by a South Carolinian to his children around the fireside in their home and written January 19, 1903.

"January 1st, 1861, I joined the Darlington Guards, with Fred F. Warley as captain. When the call came for troops, our company, with eighty-one men, was the first to reach Charleston. We were mustered into the State Confederate service. The next day we dined at the hotel, then went right over to Sullivan's Island. We remained there several months, and then went to Morris Island. The 9th of April 'The Star of the West' attempted to run the blockade to bring provisions and men to Robt. Anderson in Fort Sumter. I was on duty that night and saw the first shot fired at 'The Star of the West.' When the time that we had enlisted for was up, Captain Warley took those who stayed with him home. A good many of our company joined Colonel Maxey Gregg's regiment and went to Virginia.

Then Colonel Wilds formed a company and I joined it. We went to Georgetown and were stationed there a long time. Then the companies were reorganized, and again some came home and some went to Virginia.

The next company I joined was Company I, of the Sixth S.C. Cavalry, with J.N. Whitner as captain. This was one of Hampton's regiments. We were stationed at Green Pond, between Charleston and Savannah, on the coast, and we were there about six months, guarding the coast. Then we were sent to Columbia, where our troops was reviewed. We were there for a few days and were sent to Richmond, a journey of twenty-one days. After resting a few days, we were ordered to the front in a big battle at Seven Pines, the 11th or 12th of June 1862.

Next came the battle of Trevillian, the biggest and most fiercely contested cavalry battle of Northern Virginia.

Generals Hampton, Butler and Fitzhugh Lee, with four thousand men, and General Sheridan, with eight thousand—it was a grand sight with both armies drawn up in line of battle. Sheridan's men began to dismount to fight with muskets. We were quickly ordered to dismount, and every fourth men to take the horses to the rear. I was counted as the fourth, but, as Lide Law, my younger cousin, hadn't been in service long, I handed him the reins and took this place in battle.

Our generals had to retreat the first day, across an old field. Here Hart-well Hart was wounded and died in a few days. The next day we formed a line about two miles long. General Sheridan charged over our lines, and about 2 o'clock he was forced to retreat. We followed them and could hear thousands of axes cutting down trees to keep our troops at a distance. A minnie ball went through my horse, and, as he staggered, I got down to see what the trouble was. A comrade rode up and told me to jump up behind him. I did, and we rode this way for three or four hundred yards. Then we came across a loose horse and started off, but soon found that my horse was so badly string-halted he could hardly go. Soon I came across an old mule and captured him, and went on with the company. We pursued the Yankees to the James River. A note was handed to General Hampton. We were halted and told that the Yankees had thrown up breastworks in the woods. I expected all to be killed, as we had to cross quite an open space. The Yankees shot too high and only six of the men of our company were killed. The Yankees shelled us. Evander McIver and I crawled behind a huge log and when we came out I am sure I could have picked up my hat full of empty shells lying around the log.

Two members of our company were sent home for more horses. Then we joined General Hampton in Columbia. Next we went to Fayetteville and found the Yankees camping near a creek. Under General McIver Law we mounted and charged into their camp at sunrise, drove them all out—most of them were in their underclothes—(General) Kilpatrick himself was. Knight Gibson, one of our boys, captured Kilpatrick's fine horse. We plundered their camp, taking their cannons, provisions and everything we could find. We had another skirmish in the town of Fayetteville. We had to retreat. Our men, passing over the bridge, put turpentine on it and burned it, so the Yankees couldn't follow. I was taken sick and was sent to the Pettigrew Hospital in North Carolina. I had typhoid fever—was unconscious for weeks. One day, when I was better, I looked out of the window and saw Yankees all around. I couldn't imagine what had happened, and the nurse told me that the companies had surrendered. I was nursed by an old lady named Yates, and she was indeed kind to me.

The Yankees had taken possession of the hospital, and wanted it for their men, so as soon as I was well enough, with two men from Sumter, we were paroled and put on the train, which took us as far as Chesterfield—couldn't run any further, for the roads were cut.

So we decided to walk home, but I was so weak I didn't think I could hold out, but my comrades were kind and said that if I would try they would try they would wait on me, if we were a month on the road. So we started and walked for four days, and finally reached Mr. Bass's house, in the upper part of Darlington County. He knew my father, so loaned us a horse and buggy to come home in. In the meanwhile my father had gotten uneasy and had sent William Zimmerman, with Allen, my colored servant, in an old dray to Chesterfield to hunt me, and when I got home father telegraphed them at Chesterfield that I had arrived safely. I received a very warm welcome. All the darkies came out of the field to see me."

N.   SERGEANT JOHN GILL

Co. A, Maryland Cavalry. Attached to Second Virginia Cavalry Hq.
Fitzhugh Lee's Cavalry Division (Courier)
Cavalry Corps, ANVA

The following reminiscences of John Gill of Baltimore, Maryland, were written in 1904. They are prefaced by the remarks of General Fitzhugh Lee concerning the wartime services of the then Sergeant John Gill, a member of the General's staff.

The sergeant's recollections are those of his experiences at the Battle of Trevilian Station, June 11-12, 1864.

"Richmond, Va., March 22, 1904

John Gill, of Baltimore, served at my headquarters and near my side for the greater part of the war from 1861 to 1865. He was one of a number of heroic Marylanders who left their homes to join and do service in behalf of the South.

I had him detailed to report to me because I had been informed that he was a good soldier and performed all the duties confided to him in a satisfactory manner. I first assigned him to duty as a courier, and afterwards promoted him to be Sergeant in the Division Signal Corps. I found him active, vigilant, energetic and courageous in the various encounters between my command and the Federal Cavalry. I am correctly quoted as having stated years ago that I would be glad to lead in a fight 5,000 men like John Gill against 10,000 of the enemy.

He should know what he is writing about, because whenever the opportunity occurred his place in the war picture was near the flashing of the guns.

Fitzhugh Lee,
Formerly Major-General
Commanding Cavalry Corps
of the Army of Northern Virginia''

John Gill

"I was called to Gen. Fitz Lee's headquarters as a courier in the fall of 1863. The General's Headquarters at that time was about three miles distant from Fredericksburg, Va., at Guest's house, on the old plank road. I suppose I was indebted for this slight elevation to Capt. Henry Lee, brother of Gen. Fitz Lee, a classmate of mine at the University of Virginia prior to the war.

Shortly after the fighting around Mine Run, our division went into winter quarters at Charlottesville. In the early spring of 1864 the division moved into the vicinity of Fredericksburg again.

On June the first the cavalry moved across the Chickahominy towards Seven Pines, in the vicinity of Bottoms Bridge. On June 3d there was heavy fighting all along the line.

The movement of the cavalry was so rapid in those days that it was a rare thing to find division headquarters wagons up at night. We generally made headquarters at some farmer's house, and these people, although greatly impoverished by the war, always gave us the best they had.

The following day the division was ordered to Ashland, within sixteen miles of Richmond, and here we were joined by Butler's Brigade. We learned that a large force of cavalry, under Sheridan, had encamped the night before at Atlett's, in Caroline County.

The scouts reported that Sheridan's column was marching to join Hunter in the Valley. We left Ashland on the afternoon of the 9th, and encamped that night near Trinity Church, made an early start the next morning for Frederickshall, halted there three hours, resumed the march, and encamped at night near Louisa C.H. Sheridan's cavalry encamped within three miles of us.

June 11th we were in the saddle at 3 A.M., encountered the enemy before daylight, and fighting continued throughout the day. I was in the charge that broke Custer's line and captured his headquarters wagons and Colonel Pennington's Horse Artillery.

A few years ago, while visiting Fortress Monroe, I had the pleasure of meeting General Pennington, and of informing him that on that occasion my trophy in the battle was a handsome buffalo robe. I had taken this robe from Pennington's wagon, and I laughingly remarked that, if he still wanted it, there was a lady in Richmond by the name of Miss Mason who would doubtless return it to him.

I also had the pleasure of talking to Captain Green, Custer's adjutant-general, who was captured in this fight, and to whom I extended some slight service on the battle-field.

Some years afterwards I had the pleasure of meeting him in Baltimore. He recalled my kindness to him, remembered my name, and came into my office to meet and thank me again.

Trevilians was a desperate encounter, with varying success to both sides, but finally terminated in Sheridan's retreat.

Hampton followed him in hot pursuit. Our division, however, moved into Trevilians Station the next morning to find a large number of prisoners and wounded men left on the field. Orders were given to establish a hospital and to see that the men received proper attention. Their friends had left them to our care.

That night, after a march of nearly twenty miles, we encamped again in the vicinity of Frederickshall. In speaking of the battle of Trevilians, I am reminded of many sad memories. Up to this time in almost every engagement in which we fought, we had been successful. We had whipped and routed the enemy upon many a field. Now the tide was turning. No longer had we the men, horses or provender with which to make this branch of the service effective. The history of the cavalry of the Army of Northern Virginia, under Stuart, Hampton and Lee, will, however, stand forever distinguished for its many achievements.

General Sheridan, with inexhaustible resources, was daily adding to his magnificently equipped corps. From this time on we had no means of maintaining our former efficiency. Sheridan was indefatigable, never idle. Within two days we learned he was again on the move. It was almost impossible to keep up with him, and we were on the lookout day and night. The whole line of march was perfumed with dead horses.''

O.   SERGEANT B.J. HADEN

Co. E, First Virginia Cavalry
Wickham's Brigade, Fitzhugh Lee's Division, ANVA

Below is an excerpt from the reminiscences of Sergeant B.J. Haden of Fluvanna County, Virginia. As his story begins, his regiment is with General J.E.B. Stuart's forces which were in pursuit of Union General Philip Sheridan's troopers on their Richmond raid.

"I reached Taylorsville with more prisoners than I started with. I suppose there must have been stragglers that fell in with the column as we marched. From this point our march was continued due east until we struck the Telegraph road, then turning to the right towards Richmond, gaining Sheridan's front, who was traveling the old Mountain road, at Yellow Tavern. Here followed a series of engagements at different points. General Lomax made the attack immediately in front nearest Yellow Tavern, the First Regiment being sent to reinforce him; but before we reached him his line was broken, and the enemy charging with a heavy force, caused all to retire hastily. It was at this point, while standing upon a bank overlooking the road where there was a sudden crook, that General Stuart received a mortal wound. I had been by his side not a minute before he fell, but considering it an unhealthy place, had retired. Sheridan after finding that he was foiled in his attempt to capture Richmond moved off and rejoined the army, which was still continuing its flank movements toward Richmond, but as there was but little use for a cavalry in that vicinity, he conceived the thought of a raid upon Charlottesville, but our scouts, who were ever on the alert, informed General Hampton, who was now in command since the death of General Stuart, of their movements. He started immediately with his old division to intercept them, sending orders to General Fitz, who was down between Richmond and the Chickahominy, to follow on. It was said that General Custer, who then commanded a brigade in passing the house of General Rosser's wife's father who lived in Hanover, told the General's wife that he believed he had met about all the other brigades in a hand to hand conflict, and had come out conquerer, and would be happy indeed to meet him. It so happened that they did meet, I believe the next day, at Trevilians. General Rosser not only routed him, but captured a large number of horses he had captured from some Southern brigade the second night after he had started in pursuit.

General Hampton had gotten above Louisa Court House, near Trevilians depot, and had camped for the night, while night overtook General Fitz below the Court House. The enemy came in from the direction of South Anna River on a road which intersected the one on which we were traveling just above the Court House. Thus coming in between the two commands, they were attacked in front by Hampton, and General Fitz attacked then in rear; they, in consequence, had to divide their force, but towards night they left just enough men in front of Hampton to make a fight, and with almost their whole force turned on Fitz and drove him back with considerable loss—the loss was heavy especially in prisoners. Captain Boston's company of this county had a number of men captured, among them was Mr. Hames H. Harlow, of this county. It is right amusing to hear him tell of the affair. During the night we withdrew, and by a circuitous route through the Green Springs, joined Hampton the next day in front of the enemy. An order of attack was made, which was for the whole force to be placed in front, occupying the railroad as a breastwork, except General Lomax, who was to move around to our left and attack their right flank, which was successfully done just as they had completed their arrangements to make an assault upon our lines. This so flustrated their plans that the attack was abandoned altogether, though they held their position until about midnight, when I, who was just in front of a store house, around which some hard fighting had been done, as the enemy had taken shelter behind the house and trees in the yard, heard the order given to mount! then forward march! We were momentarily expecting to be attacked, but in a short time were satisfied that instead of their approaching us the sound of their horses hoofs was growing less distinct. General Hampton was immediately apprised of their movements, and we expected to start in a very short time in pursuit, but to our astonishment, we were not moved until about noon the following day, and then not to follow them, but march down parallel with them to the White House. I will state here, that the question has frequently been asked me as to my idea of the generalship of Generals Stuart and Hampton. My reply has generally been that what General Stuart was going to do, he would do before General Hampton got ready. But when Hampton got ready, he was there. Stuart did his work with a rush, while Hampton never made an attack until he had made thorough preparation, and consequently, was generally successful, unless he was contending with overwhelming numbers. And while their modes of fighting were very different, I am unable to say which, in my judgment, would have accomplished the most in the end. My idea is, that when the enemy left Trevilians, General Stuart would have been on them like a duck on a June bug. And while he would have harassed them, and retarded their movements to some extent, I don't suppose that much could have been accomplished by the pursuit, as they would have selected their position whenever they stopped to engage us; thereby having the advantage in every instance.''

P. PRIVATE SAMUEL BURNS RUCKER, SR.

Co. F, Sixth Virginia Cavalry
Lomax's Brigade, Fitzhugh Lee's Division, ANVA

On January 5, 1930, at the age of eighty-five, Samuel Burns Rucker, Sr. included in his recollections of war service the following events that occurred at the Battle of Trevilian Station:

"We saw one of our head surgeons riding rapidly down the road with his sleeves rolled up and his arms all bloody from his attendance on our wounded. A soldier standing by me said that some big man had been wounded, to see one of the head surgeons coming like that.

After he had passed us, he came back in about twenty minutes with Gen. J.E.B. Stuart lying on his back badly wounded. It was a sad sight to his cavalry to see their beloved general in such a fix! The ambulance passed in ten steps of me as they carried him on to Richmond, where he died the next day.

It was late in the day when we resumed our march. Going along I saw several sacks of corn thrown out of some of the commissary wagons. I got down off my horse and put a bag of it in front of me to feed my horse. A cavalry-man always thought more of his horse than he did of himself.

Night was coming on. I was on the outside file, and during one of the stops the cavalry always have in marching, my horse must have gone into the corner of the road fence. I leaned over on my bag of corn and went to sleep, and did not wake up 'till all the cavalry had passed. It was a very dark night, but I managed to catch up with the army, which had gone into camp for the night. Not being able to find my company in the dark, I fell in with the 2nd. Va. Cavalry, of which my brother was a member. Next morning I found my company all right. We then started towards the Valley to intercept Gen. Sheridan's cavalry, which was on their way to join Gen. Hunter at Lynchburg.

We met the Yankees at Trevillians Station near Gordonsville, and after a severe fight the Yankees turned in full retreat.

I had the misfortune to be captured together with my 2nd. Lieut. George Vetch and a lot of my company. We had been dismounted and forward near an old frame house on the railroad. Below the house was a row of cabins. We placed r. r. cross ties in front of the cabin to form a breastworks. Some of my company went in the cabins and knocked out the slats so they could shoot at the Yankees should they charge us. One of my company named Funkhouser was with me on the outside of the cabin in an old broken down chimney about three feet high. There was a garden in front of us, and some of our boys were up a cherry tree eating cherries when the Yankees suddenly charged us through an old orchard in front of us. When the charge started I was sitting on one side of the chimney with my gun between my legs. The first thing I knew minnie balls were knocking dust all over. I saw one of the Yankees come out of the orchard and shoot his gun, which made such a puff of smoke that I could not see him, so I fired at the centre of the smoke. I do not know whether I hit him or not; but before I got my gun loaded the Yankees had me and Funkhouser. They just swarmed around us. An old Dutchman came up to me and swapped hats with me. My hat was new, and his was an old broad-brimmed hat split all over the top.

As soon as Funkhouser and I were captured a guard took us back to the rear at once. As he carried us across the orchard over which the Yankees had charged, there were a great many dead and wounded laying there. The wounded men cursed us for all they could think of. After they had carried us to the rear, another guard brought Lieut. Geo. Veach and a lot of our company. They laughed at me heartily when they saw the hat I had on.

On carrying us along we passed a house with several women and children in the yard. I asked the Yankee guard to let me write a letter home. He made no objection; so I wrote my mother that I was captured, but was not hurt. My mother, not hearing from me for two weeks, thought I was killed, and was much relieved on receiving my letter. 350 men of our command were captured when I was.

The night I was captured it rained very hard and I laid in a corn furrow on the wet ground and it did not make me sick. It would kill me to do that now.

We were camped near the Yankee headquarters. Orderlys were coming and going all the time. I saw one of the orderly's horses throw him head foremost on the ground.

The next morning after we were captured they started with us towards York River, from which place they sent us to Point Lookout. It took several days to get there. The weather was very hot, and all of us broke completely down at last. They had to dismount their own men and put us on their horses. They mounted one half of our 350 men at a time, and at midday; they dismounted another like number of their cavalry. Those that rode in the morning were expected to walk in the evening.

The Yankee captain told all that were real sick to get in line. Nearly all of them came forward. It made the captain so mad that he put them all in line and counted off what he needed. It was my luck to be on the right end of the line, so I got a ride in the evening also.

As I started to mount a Yankee horse, three Yankees came running to me and wanted me to ride their horse. I never knew why they did that unless that I was quite slender and would not be very heavy on their horse.

As we passed through King and Queen county, the weather was extremely warm, and a good many of our men fainted from the heat and had to be put in wagons. I had on a pair of new cavalry boots and in marching it made large blisters on my heels. I started once to take off my boots but an old Irish soldier made me get up and go on. I would like to shoot at him now!

In marching, we came to a small creek, and when we were crossing a man named Burton stopped under the bank of the creek and got away.

I wrote my father where to get my horse and stated that some man was trying to steal him. My father sent and got him, and had him there when I came from prison.

We came very nearly being recaptured twice on our way to York River. We were finally landed at Point Lookout—where we landed through a line of negroes. The first black soldiers I had ever seen!

Point Lookout is on the Chesapeake Bay, and we had the privilege of going out and bathing every day—which kept us clean. Some of the boys used to get large tubs and go out and catch crabs. I never did, as I did not like crabs. The way they caught them, was to put a piece of meat on a string and throw it in the water; the crab would seize it, and they then pulled it in.

The water at Point Lookout was awful! There was but one well fit to drink, and that was kept dry—so many drinking out of it. The rest of the wells were of Copperas water and would eat up a tin cup in two weeks.

There was a great deal of sickness. A great many of our men had measles and it seemed very fatal. I suffered a great deal with dysentery."

Selected entries from Recollections of "My War Record During the Confederacy" by Samuel Burns Rucker, Sr.

This material courtesy of Jones Memorial Library, Lynchburg, Virginia.

Q. PRIVATE NOBLE JOHN BROOKS

Co. E, Cobb's Legion (Georgia)
Young's Brigade, Hampton's Division, ANVA

The following are excerpts from the diary of Private Noble John Brooks pertaining to his activities during the Battle of Trevilian Station:

"June 9, 1864. Leave camps about 3 or 4 o'clock to go to Hanover Junction to intercept a raiding party; near Ashland turn toward Louisa C. H. and after travelling all day and a portion of the night, stop till day near the railroad where the enemy destroyed a depot and several cars. This day a year ago I was captured near Beverly's ford on the Rappahannock a sharp shooting. 10th. Leave camps early and pass Bumpers Station, and Frederick Hall and stop awhile at Louisa C. H. Where we learn that the enemy were near. Late in the evening proceed 5 or 6 miles on the road to Gordonsville where the brigade stops for the night. I am sent on picket on the above road have the reserve at Mr. Gentry's house. Nothing of importance transpires during the night. 11th. About 10 or 11 o'clock we are suddenly surprised by a stampede of a portion of the 7th Ga. Cav. who were charged upon and hotly pursued by a party of Yankees. We mounted in stanter and tried to stop them but could not. Capt. Bostie drew his sabre and threatened to cut them into, but it did no good—about this juncture two of them ran against me with such force as nearly dismounted me and caused me to drop my gun, which I got down to get and the Yankees coming up at full speed fired into us which excited my horse so I could not remount. I turned him loose and jumped over in a railroad cut for safety—as they passed I heard one say 'We are giving them fits now,' but the joke was soon turned for our pickets farther on the road fired into them and turned them back. They retreated as fast as they advanced. The rear most man dismounted and fired a shot back in five feet of me. I was in a work shop by the road peeping through a crack at him. I had no arms or I would have taken him. Late in the evening they charged us again when they were repulsed with the loss of 3 killed and three horses, several were wounded but made their escape. 12th. Remain quiet until evening when a fierce engagement takes place of 3 or 4 hours duration when the enemy retire and we care for our wounded, among them Ajt. Jones of our Regt. (Cobb's Ga. Legion) who was wounded in the right shoulder by a piece of shell. About 10 or 11 o'clock P.M. go to the rear and graze horses, and lie down to sleep about midnight. 13th. 7 o'clock quietly grazing our horses. We are hungry having not had anything since yesterday morning. We have not learned anything of Win Moss, whom we lost the 11th. We found his mare which was badly wounded, nor I have not found my horse yet. About an hour after writing the above I found Win Moss and my horse which he had found and taken care of. We follow up the enemy's retreat who began to retreat last night leaving their dead and wounded behind; as I rode over the field saw a great many dead—mostly all shot in the head and breast and been stript by our men a very barbarous act. Saw <u>Col. McAllister of the 7 Ga. Cav.</u> lying by the road <u>dead</u> and a squad of men digging his grave.* The road was strewn with dead horses which had broke down and were killed by the enemy. Stop for the night in 7 miles of Bumpas's Station.''

With permission. Selected entries from the Noble Brooks Diary, #3353, Southern Historical Collection, Library of the University of North Carolina at Chapel Hill.

---

*See picture of grave of Colonel J.L. McAllister on page 26.

R.   COLONEL JOSEPH FREDERICK WARING

Commander, Jeff Davis Legion (Mississippi), Young's Brigade, Hampton's Division, ANVA

These short passages from Colonel Frederick Waring's diary covering the three days of action at the Trevilian Station battlefield give his concise view of the engagement.

"June, Friday 10, 1864

Cool, cloudy.

Began march at 2 A.M. Caught up with the front Brigade. Marched all day long, reaching Louisa C. H. at 3 P.M. Here we watered our horses, the first time in 24 hours. The Yankees are said to be on the other side of the North Anna. A party of them crossed & visited Bumpass' Station, robbing Bumpass of two horses. Our movement they did not discover till this afternoon, near Trevellyan Station. They came very near to Louisa C. H. But did not advance on Louisa to-day. We are camping near one another, & I suppose we will meet the enemy tomorrow. Butler camps between Louisa & Trevellyan's. We are near Trevellyan's. The 7th. marches very badly. They gallop too much. McAllister & Anderson are determined to do something with them. Our corn has helped out the horses in their long marches in spite of the weight.

"June, Saturday 11, 1864

Clear, warm.

We moved towards Trevellyan Station and dismounted a good many men to support Gen. Butler, who engaged the enemy early this morning. McAllister behaved splendidly. Put Ned Anderson in myself with his skirmishers. Gen. Custer flanked our position, got into our rear, & charged our train & led horses. Hampton ordered me to move back and charge the Yankees with a small body of men. We charged the enemy & were in turn charged by the enemy in our rear. Turned off to the right, crossed the rail road & moved up to get to Gen. Hampton. Found Chew up there with his guns. Saw the Yankees march off with our train, but the Artillery was so completely bare of support that I stayed with it. Was put in command of a portion of a Carolina Regiment for a short time. The men behaved very well under a heavy fire. In the afternoon we spent the time in hunting a lot of Yankees we had cut off. We have captured a good many.

Clear, cool.

Gen. Hampton selected a position commanding the Gordonsville & Charlottesville roads & we put up some field works by means of rails. Everything was quiet till three o'clock. About 12 M. the enemy were discovered endeavouring to turn our left flank. At 3 P.M. our left was furiously attacked. From that time till 8:30 P.M. a perfect fusillade was kept up. But the attempt was vain on the part of the enemy. The firing was like that from a line of battle. Thompson's battery behaved splendidly. His colour bearer sat on his horse waving his flag until shot down. A terrible fire was poured into the gunners, but they repaid the Yankees with canister, & ran all back except a few sharp-shooters. One single piece shot, two men killed, & four wounded. Immediately after night fall the Yankees began their retreat. The Carolinians fought well.

Clear & cool.

Our skirmishers advanced at sunrise & pressed forward to Trevellyan's but the Yankees were gone. Met Ned Anderson. He had been wounded and captured. He made his escape this morning. One hundred and seventy nine of the 7th Ga. were captured. The Yankees got Three hundred and eighty of our men. We captured more of their men by a good deal. There are a great many Yankee dead from yesterday's fight. Butler's Brigade & a part of Young's did all the fighting of yesterday, till near sundown, when Wickham's men were put in, but scarcely engaged the enemy. The Yankees began their retreat at midnight, the trains, however, began to move at dark. We pursued the Yankees to the North Anna. We afterwards marched along their flank. We are camping near Colman's, six miles from Frederick Hall.

Clear, cool.

Our horses came in last night to find nothing to eat. This morning we sent out & got plenty of clover but no corn. Mr. Sheridan gets away from us without further fight by reason of the exhausted condition of our horses.

About mid day we moved to the wood near our old camp on Gen. Coleman's place near Frederick Hall. Col. Dalgren told him that he knew me intimately. He must resemble his cousin Charles, I suspect. Dalgren's sister was the prettiest girl I ever saw. We grazed."

NOTE: "The 7th" he refers to was the Seventh Georgia Cavalry. Colonel J.L. McAllister of this unit was killed. A picture of his grave and marker is shown on page 26. The name "Chew" he refers to was Major R.P. Chew who commanded the artillery battalion and "Thompson" commanded one of the artillery batteries. "Ned Anderson" was Lt. Colonel E.C. Anderson of the Seventh Georgia Cavalry.

With permission. Selected entries from the Joseph Frederick Waring Diary, #1664, Southern Historical Collection, Library of the University of North Carolina at Chapel Hill.

S.   FIRST SERGEANT CHARLES PAINE HANSELL

Co. E, Twentieth Battalion, Georgia Cavalry
Young's Brigade, Hampton's Division, ANVA

Extracts from the memoirs of First Sergeant Charles Paine Hansell about the Battle of Trevilian Station are as follows:

"Monday June 6th, we went back through Richmond to a place near Meadow Brook Bridge, where we were put in Young's Brigade and attached to the Jeff Davis Legion, Col. Fred Waring commanding, Gen. Gid. J. Wright of the Cobb Legion, in the absence of Gen. P.M.B. Young, was commanding the Brigade. Here we rested until Wednesday P.M., the 8th of June. Then we were issued about three or four days rations and ordered to cook them up and I, as 1st Serg., was called upon to report the number of men and horses fit for duty, and it seemed to me that some additional information was asked for every half hour or less between sun down and midnight. About 2 A.M. 'boots and saddles' was sounded and we were soon in the saddle prepared for a trip of some kind. There were three of my men to go, Guyte Fondren, Frank Winn, and myself, and we could find but one haversack, so the biscuits, of which there seemed a large number, were put in the wallet and the meat in the haversack. As my horse was the smallest I took the meat and the others the wallet of biscuits, a bad arrangement for all of us, as it turned out. These two comrades, never having known what it was to deny themselves of anything and raised in abundance, they just helped themselves whenever they felt like it, with the result, on Friday about noon, when I asked for a biscuit there was but one left in the wallet. We got away before day and rode steadily all day. One little incident that occurred soon after the sun was up impressed upon me the fact that our gallant and heroic commander, Gen. Wade Hampton, was not only a great General, but a most perfect gentleman as well, and one who looked upon his soldiers as gentlemen. Our line of march was converging toward a rail fence on our right. It was seen that a party of horsemen on our left must pass through our column or be crowded against the fence in a few minutes. The one at the head of this party rode up to the head of Company E and said, in a most pleasant manner and with the softness and gentleness of a lady—'Gentlemen, let me pass please.' The men looked around and recognizing Gen. Hampton, pulled back with such vigor and earnestness as almost to throw their horses on their haunches. Had the manner and tone been other than they were, a military order instead of a request, there would have been a way made, but a very different one. We pushed along all day by roads apparently almost unused, across woods and fields occasionally, until a little before sunset, we went by a large farm house and, following a farm road across a small creek, mounted a short steep hill and entered a large field where the clover, as I remembered, had been cut. Here we halted till the artillery, one battery of the Stuart Horse Artillery, could get across the creek and come up with us. Then we waited. Did you ever have to wait in line on horseback, with a heavy gun bearing down on your shoulders by a strap, a canteen, a belt with sabre on one side and forty rounds of ounce ball cartridges on the other? Your bedding and horse felt strapped to your saddle, after 14 or 15 hours riding. We couldn't dismount without orders; your Capt. dare not give them unless the Col. said so and the Col. could not do it without orders from the General; and the General didn't dare do it, because he had no idea what minute he might have to move to hunt the enemy, or because the enemy in superior force was hunting him. But first one and then another got down without orders and as nothing was done about it others followed suit, and we munched our rations and let our horses pick about for what they could find. We couldn't unsaddle or take our blankets loose; so we tumbled down and were soon asleep. We were aroused sometime during the night by the call of the bugle. W.S. Mallard of Company E and myself had gone to sleep, his legs furnishing me a pillow, while mine did the same for him. Fortunately my horse was standing over us and his right by, and we held the bridle reins still in our hands, so that all we had to do was rub our eyes, shake ourselves, and mount. Some were not so fortunate; many calls were heard for 'my horse' and one poor boy cried out in tears; 'Where's my horse?' and was answered by a dozen different voices in as many directions; 'Here's your horse, sonny' —'don't cry, bud; here he is,' etc., etc., until he was literally at his wits end, when some comrade brought his horse to him. We soon moved out and as the stars were shining brightly we soon began to discuss the direction we were travelling. Jim Carroll from near Atlanta had spent sometime in Virginia in the infantry service and professed to know something of the country; so he was called on to tell us where we were and whither we were heading. After considering the stars carefully he came to the conclusion that we were going towards Fredericksburg; but we didn't believe it and so told him, though we had no good reason to give for our belief and he had the best of it. After daylight we found ourselves travelling a public road, the general direction of which was westerly, and the first place we found a stream of water a large number broke rank to let their horses get a drink. Maj. Lewis of the Jeff Davis Legion, being in immediate command of our Batt. gave them to understand that they must get back in ranks and stay there; but it was not long before the same thing happened again and then again. The vocabulary of 'Cuss' words was a fine one; but I think he exhausted it that day and had to repeat several times, and only the fact that he made one or two get down and walk for some distance and carry weight (a rail or something like it) finally broke up this business. Along about 4 P.M. we came to a place which we found to be Louisa Court House, a village of possibly 500 inhabitants, about 60 miles from Richmond on the Virginia Cen. R.R., now the C and O. Somebody went down an alley to an ice house and rode back with a piece of ice in his mouth, water melting from which made two streaks of white, one on each side of his mouth where it washed off the red dust that had been collecting all day and was then nearly 1/8th of an inch thick all over any portion of his anatomy that was not covered. His appearance caused a laugh at his expense; but very many more followed his example and returned in the same general condition. After a short rest we passed on along the road to Trevilian Station. About a mile or two out someone reported that there were Yankees at Louisa Court House and the gallant Col. MacAllister of the 7th. Ga. Cav. went galloping back to see for himself if it were true. We halted till his return and then moved on and camped for the night a short distance beyond Trevilian's. The 7th. Ga. Regt. Cav. has been organized at Savannah by the combination of 3 Batts. and had joined us the day before we started on this trip. It was said to number 800 men mounted, and that 750 of this number came on this trip. Its field officers were Col. MacAllister, Lt.-Col. E.C. Anderson, Jr. and Major Russell. The next morning, Saturday, June 11th, at an early hour this Regt. was formed in the pike near us, and I there recognized Capt. Frank W. Hopkins by his resemblance to others of his family then in Thomasville. They moved off down the pike over the same route we hade come the P.M. before and in a few minutes the rest of the Brig. followed. We left the pike and turned square off to the left or northward, rode by a large two story house, through a small piece of woods, and then halted and remained here for sometime, sitting on our horses and listening to the firing in front where the 7th dismounted and Butler's Brig. were engaging the enemy, and listening with still sharper interest at the singing of the minie balls as they went over or by us at short intervals. While waiting here quite a number of prisoners passed on by going to the rear and some wounded man. Anyone who has been situated just that way or anywhere that the minies were whistling can tell you that even an ordinary horse feels like he might be 15 feet instead of 15 hands high. After a while, much to my relief, our squadron was ordered to dismount and report to Capt. Jimmie Nichols of the Phillip Legion. This gallant and clever officer led us through the woods and across a small field to the fence nearest to where the fight seemed to be progressing. We could not see any distance in front of us because the woods were too thick. We had scarcely taken our position behind this fence when we were ordered to fall back. We returned to where we had dismounted and Capt. Nichols mounted his men and left us, we were told to mount and did so, but were at a loss where to go. I learned afterwards that just after we left, it was reported that the Yankees were in our rear and the rest of the Brig. wheeled about and rode for the pike; but as they reached there they found themselves in the midst of Custer's Brigade of Federals and most of them were captured. Meanwhile, sitting on our horses, through an opening in the woods we had a fine view of the charge made by Rosser's Brig. which had gone towards Gordonsville the night before and, being recalled by Gen. Hampton, came down in time to strike Custer and, in a headlong charge, drive him back and recapture nearly all of ours that he (Custer) had captured a few minutes before. It was certainly a grand and most gratifying thing to us to watch this, but meanwhile what were we to do? Just then our friend, Maj. Lewis, rode up and took command and ordered us to go forward toward the pike by the same route we first came in; but we had scarcely started, however, when he halted us and galloped off by himself toward the pike. As soon as he was gone, we, not realizing our perilous position, had let our reins loose and our horses were biting at leaves and grass. The Major returning at gallop called out: 'You d--d fools, what you mean by grazing your horses and the Yankees right on! Form fours, draw sabres, and if you get out of this you'll have to eat your way out.' With this he lead us back to the opening and as we passed I recognized the 7th Ga. lined up along the road at a rest and we passed almost in touching distance of the right of their line. These men were soon afterwards all captured, while if they had known enough about battles to have double-quicked after us they might many, if not all, have escaped that time. Meanwhile, as we rode around the woods and saw no Yankees between us and the pike, I began to feel better and see a way of escape without charging through a line of blue-coated horsemen. A little further on I saw to our right and in front what was left of one of our batteries, where the men were stripping the harness of their dead and wounded horses, and evidently preparing to get away while the shells from a Yankee battery to our left, but out of sight, were dropping around them. Lieut. Tom Heeth of Company A was at that time in charge of Company D in our squadron, which had no commissioned officer on hand, and just as we drew near this place he rode up near me and remarked: 'Charlie this looks like a mighty tight place.' So far as I have been able to learn those were his last words, as he was not seen again and his horse and saddle all bloody ran out and rejoined Company A, where he was caught. The rest of us passed through safely and, reaching the pike at a place on a line with our battery, were halted and remained sitting there on our horses, with our backs towards the enemy, for some time while the shells fell and exploded to our right. A Battn. of Virginians coming up from our rear raised a dust and the artillery, knowing that meant a moving column, fired a shell into it. As we stopped in the road I had found a riderless horse with all his equipments standing by me and I caught his bridle and pulled him up along side and was examining him to see if it would pay to swap. I decided that it was probably a 7th Ga. and not a Yankee horse, when the shell above alluded to or one from same source burst just in front of us and split his head from nose to ears. I was either stunned by the shock of the explosion or too scared to know exactly what I was doing and started forward and rode out of the road and few steps forward when the voice of Major Lewis asking; 'Where are you going Srgt?' recalled me to myself and I reined up and started back, when the Major said: 'No, come on we will leave here,' and we rode on. That same shell killed two or three of the Virginians and cut through the right arm of Priv. Wm. M. Hayes, better known as Billie, between the elbow and shoulder and threw him from his horse. Regaining his feet he looked around and spied Gen. Hampton and staff on their horses a little way off. He was then about 18 yrs. of age, but being short and with a smooth, beardless, round face did not look more than 15. He had no shock or unconsciousness from the wound, and, with impudence that was one of his prime characteristics then, he walked boldly up to Gen. Hampton and said: 'Gen., I want my arm attended to.' The General turned to Dr. Watt Taylor, the chief Medical Officer of the Division, and told him to take that boy and attend to his arm. The Dr. took to a tree near by and Dr. Jno. Mobley, Hospital Steward, of our Batt. coming up, they took Billie and found that his arm must be amputated at the shoulder. As the shells were still dropping around there, they hailed an ambulance and put him in. Instead of lying down, Billie took the front seat and Dr. Mobley sat behind him, holding the main artery between his fingers. The driver of the ambulance and the mules were all badly frightened and Hayes, taking the whip from the driver, lashed the mules and drove them away from there. Later in the day I met some friends in another Company of ours and they asked who was hurt and I told them Billie Hayes had an arm shot off. They said that could not be, as they saw him go by in the ambulance as bright and cheery as anyone could be. Hayes told me, not many months afterward, that he did not know he was much hurt, and as they went through a lot of captured Yanks, one of them said: 'Buddie won't you have some chicken?'

and he replied—'You G--D-- blue-bellied son of a ---, I wouldn't have anything you've got!' The Dr. then told him that he had better be thinking of the other world, as he had a fair chance of getting there soon. The last I knew of Billie he was a prominent preacher of the M. E. Church South and had been a preacher for many years. To return to my part—Major Lewis lead us on down the road until we had climbed a hill and gone down on the other side, well out of range of these shells, and halted. We had been here only long enough to realize what a relief it was to be out of range, when, turning to me, he said: 'Sergt., go back yonder and see if any of your men are still there.' That looked hard, very hard. We had just left the place because it was too dangerous to stay there; but orders must be obeyed; so setting spurs to my horse I started back, went over the hill and then down the road where I knew I was in view of those artillery fellows in blue, though I could not see them. I went far enough to see the place distinctly and saw no one there; but looking to my right, I saw Capt. Paine, Frank Winn, and Leonard Sims, and one other that I cannot now recall, making from that place across a field toward a wood, but only so short a distance from the point I was to go back to, that I knew they had not been long away from it. I became interested in them and turned off the road and went to them. I saw Capt. Paine was limping and asked him if he was wounded. He said, no, but his leg was hurt by the fall of his horse. I dismounted and insisted on his taking my horse, which he refused to do. Sims, who was one of our 'old men,' that is, he was 45 or maybe 46 years of age, said he was faint and dizzy. I then insisted that he ride. He mounted and rode a few steps, when he dismounted, with the remark that he was so dizzy he was afraid he would fall off. I saw a hollow that looked like it might have a branch and suggested that we go there. As we turned a shot whistled between us and the others and they turned away from it to their right and we to our left, toward the place where I expected to find the water. This turned us back somewhat in the direction of where the Yankee lines might be. Sims had no arms of any kind, and my gun had no cap on it, so was virtually useless. Just as we came near a row of bushes, an old hedge row, a Yankee Srgt. with a pistol in hand raised up and demanded our surrender. I was fully impressed at once with the idea that we had run on a Yankee line and that there were others behind the hedge, obeyed his orders and surrendered. I have always felt ashamed of this little incident, believing that I ought to have ordered him in and that he would have come. He ordered us to come around through a gap in the hedge row and when we stepped through found the Yank was alone; but then he had us covered with his six shooter. I handed him my gun and he broke the stock and threw the gun

120

away. He was very anxious to know where our lines were; but we refused to tell for one good reason, we didn't know. He then said, 'If I get you to our lines you are my prisoners, but if I run into your lines, I am your prisoner.' We, of course, agreed; because we couldn't help ourselves and, also, because it gave us new hope in that it showed he was lost. We started along the road toward the pike and I began to scheme to give Sims the wink, grab the fellow's pistol and capture our captor, but I had hardly conceived the idea when, off to our right, we heard the clatter of hoofs and rattle of sabres. I said: 'There are your men now!' 'No,' he says, 'They are yours!' 'Give me that pistol,' I replied. 'All right,' said he, 'I'm your prisoner.' A squad of Virginians came up at a gallop hollering 'surrender!' 'surrender!' I said: 'That's right, he's my prisoner.' They surrounded us and took possession of the Srgt., claiming the right to 'go through him,' which they proceeded to do most thoroughly; but allowed me to keep the pistol, belt, & cartridge box attached. Sims had recovered his breath by this time and we all went on together until we got back to where I spied some of the 20th and joined them. I found several of our Company and Capt. Paine in a few minutes and came up with H. Frank Jones, Adjutant of the Cobb Legion, and we sat on our horses and laughed over the many ridiculous things that had happened that morning. Dick Stapler of Company A came along with a hat that started in a point in the crown and gradually widening was more than a foot long, with no brim, very like the ones the clown in a circus usually wears. Dick had been captured when our Brig. charged into Custer's and a Yank had taken his cap and given him this hat. Very soon after he was recaptured, when Rosser made his charge, and had appropriated a good hat from a Yankee, but kept the other as a curiosity. Frank Jones told us how our wagon of medical stores had been captured and the Yanks rolled out a barrel of whiskey that was in it and shot holes in the barrel and were filling their canteens when our men came upon them and captured them, and then proceeded to fill up their canteens from the barrel. While we were laughing over this, a member of the Cobb Legion came up and, producing a canteen with some of the liquor in it, offered it. While we were talking three men on horse back approached from the direction where Rosser's men were still holding the enemy in check. Two, of them seemed to be holding the third one, who wore a Lt. Col's uniform, on his horse. Capt. Paine thinking the Col. was badly wounded rode over to them and offered to help; but from the laugh with which he was greeted and a closer inspection, found the Col. had only imbibed too freely from that barrel. We spent sometime here in pleasant conversation, the last we were ever to have with Adjt. Frank Jones, as he was killed the next day, or rather so badly wounded that he died

121

Monday. Our brigade was so badly scattered that it was not until late in the afternoon that the various portions of it were gotten together and we were then marched westward a half mile or so and went into camp. I then realized that I was very hungry, not having had anything like a square meal since the morning of Friday, and had nothing to satisfy that hunger except some raw meat. After our horses had been attended to, Frank Winn said there was a mill back on the road where he thought we could buy some flour. So we slipped away without telling anyone of our intentions. We found the Mill without any trouble and in a house attached to it found a lady who sold us the flour we asked for, at a reasonable price, for the money then in use. As we had no cooking utensils we asked her if she couldn't cook it for us. She declared she had been cooking all day and was too tired to do any more; but I suppose we must have looked both the disappointment and the hunger we felt, for she relented, took the flour and made up a dough that she rolled out thin and slapped on a griddle before the fire and told us when to turn the hoe cakes. They cooked the fastest and disappeared the quickest of any hoe-cake I ever saw. After a time, after the first edge was taken off his appetite, Frank said: 'Charlie, I've got some buttermilk here.' I replied: 'Why didn't you speak sooner: but pass it over.' After we had eaten about enough for three or four, it occurred to us there were some very hungry friends in camp, so we saved up a part and carried it to camp and divided it up, reserving only a small piece each, about 2 x 5 inches for breakfast. The next morning, Sunday, June 12, '64, we rose pretty early, and after making our toilets, which consisted of pulling our shoes out from under our heads and putting them on our feet and then putting on our coats, we proceeded to clean our house by rolling up our blankets and strapping them to our saddles and we were ready to vacate the premises. We were soon mounted and rode back to a point where a road left the pike going northward, and we turned into this and went a short distance up it and were ordered to halt and dismount. Capt. Paine not being equal to walking, I took charge of the nine men constituting Company E and three or four from Company D, and went to a house between this road and the woods beyond this house. I was sent with Sims and Baggs of Company E and Billy Lee, Hyers, and Perry of Company D., to a place on the left of the house as we faced the woods, just beyond the yard, and on the side of the garden fence, to a small potato house built of logs and being about 2½ or 3 feet high and then with a roof, the comb of which was about 5 feet above ground. Along side of this we built a rail pile, but not as good or high as it ought to have been; but it was hot and the men tired, so we quit with that about 2 or 2½ feet high: then an opening 3 or 4 inches wide to shoot through, and a rail above to protect our heads while fighting. In front of us the ground sloped downward for about half or more of the distance, some 300 yards or more between us and a rail fence that bounded the open field, and back of the fence was a thick oak woods; to our left and front the same open field continued to a point where it reached the R.R. at a little two story white house. Soon after everything was arranged and while we were taking it easy waiting for the attack, I was called back to the house, or yard rather, and received an order to send a detail of a Sgt. and two men to report to someone—don't remember who, for some special duty. Corp. Seymour Smith was standing by me when the order was received. I turned to him and said 'Seymor, take D. Martin and—(cannot recall the other man's name) and report for this duty.' To my surprise he said that he would not go. I expressed my surprise at such a refusal and he then explained that as the order was for a Sgt. and he was not a Sgt. I could not force him to go. I did not see my way clear, in the face of his refusal to act as Sgt., to disobey the letter of the order; so, turning to Jack Hardee, the only Sgt. I had, I said: 'Jack, you will have to go,' and he said: 'All right,' and, taking the two men, went off. I mention this for the reason that Corpl. Smith was killed that evening within a yard or two of where the conversation occurred and Sgt. Hardee and his men were sent to do vidette duty on our extreme left and were not under fire at all that day. How about this as an example of 'predestination' and 'free agency?' We continued to wait around until about 12:30 or 1 P.M., when suddenly, up near the R.R. and the little house, the enemy came out of the woods and over the fence with their hip! hip! hip! A good big bunch of them. A piece of artillery that was on top of the little slope back of us fired and the shell went screaming over and exploded in that group of blue coated gentry. By the time the smoke cleared away there was not a Yankee to be seen; they were all back under cover of the woods. The artillery men did not fire another shot and for what seemed to us an hour we heard nothing from them. I had somehow gotten it into my head that we were ordered not to fire until the enemy came over the fence; so, when they began their attack up near to and beyond the little station (R.R.) house and at the same time commenced firing from along the fence at us and at the artillery men in our rear, I made my squad hold their fire. This got so warm for the artillery that a Lieut. galloped down near me and asked why we did not fire. I replied that I understood our orders were not to fire until 'those people'came over the fence. He replied that I was mistaken and he would stand for its being all right; so we began firing at the smoke of the guns. The men were cool and deliberate and took careful aim with each shot; but despite this, it was not a great while before our ammunition, 40 rounds to the man, began to run short, and I sent Corpl. Billie Lee back for more. As Corpl. Lee came back down the slope toward us, it was evident the enemy could see him, as the bullets knocked up the dust in front of and all around him; but he only pulled down the brim of his hat over his face, as one does when facing a rain and came on to us. I distributed the ammunition, 40 rounds more to the man, and we continued firing. After a little Wm. A. Baggs from Liberty County, a man about 45 yrs. of age, was struck on the knee, not seriously wounded; but I told him he had better get back to the rear. In getting back he was shot again and this time mortally wounded and died that night, or the next morning. Soon after Baggs left us our Adjt. Thos. G. Pond, came over to see us to see how we were getting along. He had no arms but his pistol and I told him to go on back that we did not need him. He knelt down behind our little breastwork built of rails, in just the same place Baggs had occupied. I told him that he had better get away from there or that fellow would get him. Our pile was a space between the main pile of rails and the top rail. The Adjt. rested his head against the top rail and looked through the opening for a minute or two when a ball came along and cut a piece out of the top rail almost touching his head. I again told him to get away; but had hardly said so, when another cut out another piece of the same rail just a little nearer his head. He then decided I was right and left. A few minutes later Leonard Sims, a man about the same age and size of Baggs, from East Point, Ga., moved into this place and in a few minutes a ball struck him between the collar bone and the neck. We saw he was done for, but to do what we could for him. The four of us took him up and carried him back to the chimney of the Kitchen and there gave him water and did what we could for him. I got up and, in looking around, stepped out on the side of the kitchen opposite the place we had come from, thinking there was no danger on that side. About the time I got still and looked around one of the boys called to me to move or I would be shot. I thought he was joking, but moved about a foot and as I did I heard the whistle of the bullet as it missed me. I then got behind the kitchen and Capt. Long of the Jeff Davis Legion, who had charged at that point, called to me: 'Srgt. take your men back!' I answered that we were out of ammunition. He said to come over to him: he was behind another house and he would supply me. I went over and found that the man who had been sent for the ammunition would be back in a minute. This man came running around the corner of the house in rear of the one we were behind, and as he came around a bullet sped so close to him that it seemed a wonder he was not hit. Capt. Long gave me the ammunition and I threw it across to the man behind the kitchen and then, having filled my own cartridge box, ran across to the men; told them to come on; and ran as far as the tree, when, finding no one with me, stopped behind that and called to the others to come on. No one came and after a while I went back and, finding no place to shoot from, went into the main dwelling and went in the basement and bought two glasses of buttermilk from an old negro woman for $1.00. The Adjt. came and called me to come with him as he had a good place for me. We went back to the back of the main dwelling and between this and the corner, he told me, was a good place. I asked how far he thought it was to the fence where the enemy were. He said: '300 yards.' I said it was nearer 500; but set my sight for 300 and told him to watch. We both saw the ball knock up the dust before it reached the fence. I then put the sight up to 500 yds. and fired and this time we did not see it strike. He then asked me to let him shoot. He did so. By this time I presume the smoke had attracted the attention of the fellows we were shooting at and just as he fired a spent ball struck him square on the shin and he threw the gun to me and went off hopping on one foot. I was sorry for him, but having seen that the ball did not go in I could not help stopping to laugh. It was then growing dusk and the boys raised a yell and I ran around and joined a crowd around the tree. I fired from there once or twice and then the ball stuck a little more than half down and I was unarmed. I ran out by the kitchen and there met the Adjt., who called me to fall in and we would go over to the main line where we were much needed. I told him I was no good as I had no gun. 'Oh, come on and you can wait until some fellow is killed and take his,' he replied. I didn't like the prospect but started with him. I came across a fellow on horseback and stopped to beg his gun and when I looked around the Adjt. and his crowd of 8 or 10 were out of sight in the dark and I returned to the house and found several of the 20th Batl. there, engaged in burying Dr. Wm. Stegall of Company F. and Corp. Seymor Smith of Company E. This was my first experience in this line and it was sad business. The tools we had were very poor and the ground very hard and rocky; so the grave was not very deep and it was hard to shovel the dirt right back on them with nothing like a coffin to keep it off their bodies. It had been dark some time before this melancholy task was finished, and the firing and all ceased and everything was quiet. Soon we began to hear in front of us the rumbling of artillery wheels and of wagons and we believed the enemy were moving; but we had no orders to advance and spent the night on watch around where we had fought. The next morning, very soon after light, the orders came to move forward and we went across to the corner where the Yanks first came over the fence. We found that corner almost covered with the enemy's dead. We turned around to our right into the open space beyond the woods from which they had fired upon us the day before and here we found every evidence that the enemy had left in a hurry. Fires were burning or rather smouldering here and there and on rails piled so as to keep them off the ground, we found several quarters of freshly butchered beef, some cracker crumbs, and a little butter. I could eat raw bacon, but could not go raw beef without bread, and watched with envy Joe B. Holst of my company cut off great pieces of round steak and throw them on the coals for a minute and then gulp them down. I ate what cracker crumbs I could get that seemed at all clean. We waited here until our horses came up and along with them came Danl. Martin, one of the men I had sent off on picket the day before, who beckoned from his horse to me. I went to him and he pulled out a cracker about 2½ ins. square and pushed it into my hand, saying: 'Srgt., I have been saving this for you and you must take it.' Though the cracker was so hard it was next to impossible to eat it, I think I must have gnawed on it for an hour or more; yet I have always held in grateful remembrance his kindness in thus dividing what must have been a very scanty store; for rations were all out with everyone and a man would have given all he could raise in the way of money for one square meal. My horse had for some reason been left behind so I mounted Sims' (he had been killed the day before) and went back for mine and then learned, for the first time, of the death of my dear friend Adjt. Frank Jones of the Cobb Legion. He was terribly wounded by a piece of shell Sunday P.M. and died Monday A.M. I found my horse after a while and also found one or two members of the Batl., and we started out to overtake the command which had gone in pursuit of Sheridan. I tried to get information from some of Lomax's men, Fitz Lee's Division, but they either didn't know or wouldn't tell. About 9 or 10 o'clock we came across a cherry tree that was loaded with fruit and every single one on it seemed to be perfectly ripe. We ate just as many as we could hold and before we had gone a half mile were very sorry we couldn't eat more. One rather disagreeable feature of this return trip was that we were following the route Sheridan went up and for miles we were never out of sight of a dead horse. Evidently as soon as a horse gave out he was lead to one side of the road and shot. Evidently they were in great haste. Yet Gen. Horace Porter in 'Campaigning with Grant' said: 'Gen. Sheridan went to Trevillian Station and, having accomplished his purpose, returned'—What purpose? Well, either Tuesday noon or Wednesday we finally got near enough to the commissary wagons to have some cooked (?) rations sent us. They consisted of hoe-cake and biscuits, the former about 10 inches in diameter and 1½ in. thick; the latter as big as a real big fist. They were cooked about so deep, top and bottom, and the rest was raw and as heavy as lead. My appetite was gone. I started in on one and the more I chewed the bigger it got. I gave it up and went off in the shade and laid down to rest. Two of the older men of my Company, A.S. Fowler and A.M. Hairstone, had kindled a fire and fried some of the bread and made some coffee and they hunted me up and brought it hot, and I ate that with great relish and was soon all right. We continued to follow Sheridan until we reached a station, Chesterfield, I think, on the road from Richmond to Fredericksburg. Here our dismounted men, that is men having no horses, from our Brigade and Gen. Butler's, came along (they were called 'Farley's Corps' by ours). I was still riding Sims' horse, a very fine animal, but its back was sore. All men whose horses were unfit for service were told to ride out of line. A large number rode out and I with them. Col. Gid. J. Wright, commanding the brigade, went along this line and made fun of us and the majority of them went back to their places, and I would have gone too, very willingly, if it had been my own horse; but I stuck it out and was told to go to Farley with my gun and cartridges, blankets, and rations, I felt loaded down and it seemed impossible for me to march and was glad the crowd halted every few minutes for rest. There was little order or discipline in Farley's Corps and I fell in with a Jeff Davis Legion man and told him I had another horse back at the 'dead line' of 'Co. Q,' as the place where disabled, sick, etc. horses and men were temporarily kept, and if I could get him would rejoin the mounted column. This new found friend said he knew if I told Col. Waring of that he would give me an order to go back after him. Although it had before seemed impossible to walk a quarter of a mile without stopping, I now struck out and followed the column until I reached it, some 8 or 10 miles; I have always thought it may have been much less.''

With permission. Selected entries from the Diary of Charles Paine Hansell, Civil War Miscellany, Personal Papers, Georgia Department of Archives and History, Atlanta, Georgia.

T.   BRIGADIER GENERAL WESLEY MERRITT, U.S.A.

Commander, Reserve Brigade, First Division
Cavalry Corps, Army of the Potomac.

The following statement by General Merritt commending an officer who fought in the Battle of Trevilian Station is quoted below:

"I have the honor to recommend that Major E.B. Williston, 3rd U.S. Artillery, be awarded, under A.R. 175, a Medal of Honor for having especially distinguished himself at the action of Trevilian Station, Virginia, June 12, 1864. Major Williston, then a lieutenant, was in command of Horse Battery D, 2nd U.S. Artillery. In the crisis of the action at Trevilian, when my lines were being pressed by an overwhelming force of the enemy, Lieutenant Williston planted three guns of his battery in an exposed but favorable position for effective work; and then personally moved the fourth gun onto the skirmish line. Using double charges of canister he, by his individual efforts, greatly aided in resisting successfully the charges of the enemy on our front. The loss of the brigade, reduced at that time in strength, was twelve (12) officers killed and wounded and two hundred and twenty-two (222) men."

In his official report of the action General Merritt waxed considerably more eloquent.

"Right gallantly did the battery come up in the midst of a heavy musketry fire, we being at that time so close to the enemy that their shells all flew far over us. Planting three guns of the battery in this position, where it dealt the enemy heavy blows, Lieutenant Williston moved one of his brass 12-pounders onto the skirmish line. In fact, the line was moved to the front to allow him to get an eligible position, where he remained with his gun, in the face of the strengthened enemy (who advanced to its very muzzle), dealing death and destruction in their ranks with double loads of canister."

When Lieutenant Williston and his gun crew moved their lone gun up in advance of the others, in front of the main line up with the skirmishers, they voluntarily placed themselves in a very perilous position in order to fire more effectively upon the advancing enemy. On the preceding day, another lone gun was exposed in a similar way.

The hero of this action was a soldier who, when Fort Sumter was fired upon in April, 1861, had already served nearly three and one-half years of a five-year enlistment. John Kennedy was born in Cavan, Ireland, on May 14, 1834. The records describe him as being five feet, seven and one-half inches tall, having red hair, blue eyes, and a ruddy complexion. It is apparent that the Kennedy family was among the many thousands who came to this country as a result of the great potato famine in Ireland and, following in the footsteps of many another Irishman who found work hard to get in the late 1850's, Kennedy had enlisted in the army.

Prior to the Civil War, his army career appears to have been fairly uneventful, although he recorded that he had been with Battery M of the 2nd U.S. Artillery on the Utah expedition of 1858. During the war, however, he had fought with his battery on many hotly contested fields. By the time of the Battle of Trevilian Station he was on his second enlistment; eventually he would serve seven enlistments and retire as an ordnance sergeant after thirty-three years of honorable service.

U.   PRIVATE DAVID CARTER RIDGEWAY

Co. D, Sixth South Carolina Cavalry
Butler's Brigade, Hampton's Division, ANVA

Twenty-nine year old Private David Carter Ridgeway was killed in the first days' engagement at the Battle of Trevilian Station. His great-granddaughter, Louise D. Tucker of Greenville, South Carolina, has provided the following information:

"Private Ridgeway, before he joined the cavalry, lived at or near Princeton, S.C. He was plowing in a field one day when he was summoned to serve in the army. He left immediately with his horse and saddle which also was drafted. The Company Muster-in Roll shows he entered on duty on May 14, 1862 at Greenville, S.C. It states the value of his horse was $150.00 and equipment at $60.00.

He came home on furlough one time and his wife Louise Caroline McDougal Ridgeway became pregnant and gave birth to Robert Carter Ridgeway who never saw his father who had given his life for his country. The trooper's wife was told her husband was killed on the platform of the train station. His body was buried and never returned home. It is assumed he was buried at the Oakland Cemetery in Louisa, Virginia. (See page 26.)

His wife raised four boys, ages 8, 5, 4 and one she was carrying. She was a little Irish lady and lived to be ninety-eight years old. She is buried at Columbia Baptist Church, Augusta Road, Rt. 3, Honea Path, S.C."

APPENDIX

German Nationals In Confederate Gray

With the greatly enhanced public interest and awareness of the impact and magnitude of the American Civil War on the social, economic and political structure of our nation, there has been a proliferation and growth of military reenactment groups. Of the thousands of reenactors who took part in the recent filming of the motion picture "Gettysburg", many of the participants were members of reenactment units from Great Britain, other European countries, Canada and Australia as well as those from all regions of our nation.

Pertinent to this is the case of the reenactment group made up of men from Bavaria, Germany, who have designated their unit the Seventh Georgia Cavalry. The Seventh Georgia Cavalry played an important role in the Battle of Trevilian Station. Its commander, Colonel J.L. McAllister, was killed in the battle and is buried in Oakland Cemetery, Louisa, Virginia. Interred beside him is Captain Hines of the same regiment. The nearly one hundred and thirty year old graves and headstones are shown on page 26.

The leader of the German group is Dusty Eisenberg of Gmund a. Teg., Germany, who visited the author recently and provided funds to have the grave markers cleaned. Sand-blasting has restored the stones to their original appearance.

Members of Germany's Seventh Georgia Cavalry Reenactment Unit are pictured below.

We are indebted to these men for their interest in, and dedication to, the memory of this noted fighting regiment of the Army of Northern Virginia, Confederate States of America.

BIBLIOGRAPHY

Abdill, George B.   *Civil War Railroads*, Seattle, Superior Publishing Co., 1961.

Allen, Stanton P.   *Down in Dixie*, Boston, L. Lothrop Co., 1888.

Baylor, George.   *Bull Run to Bull Run*, Richmond, B.P. Johnson Publishing Co., 1900.

Black, Robert C. III.   *The Railroads of the Confederacy*, Chapel Hill, The University of North Carolina Press, 1952.

Boatner, Mark M. III.   *The Civil War Dictionary*, New York, David McKay Co., Inc., 1959.

Bond, Oliver, J.   "The Story of the Citadel", 1936.

Brick, John.   *The Richmond Raid*, Doubleday & Co., N.Y., N.Y., 1963.

Brooks, U.R. (Editor).   *Stories of the Confederacy*, Columbia, The State Co., 1912.
　　　　　　　　　　　Butler and His Cavalry, Columbia, The State Co., 1909.

Bruce, Robert V.   *Lincoln and the Tools of War*, Indianapolis, Bobbs-Merrill Co., Inc., 1956.

Catton, Bruce.   *A Stillness at Appomattox*, Garden City, Doubleday & Co., Inc., 1954.

Cauthen, Charles E., *South Carolina Goes to War*, Chapel Hill, The University of North Carolina Press, 1950.

Cheney, Newell.   *History of the Ninth Regiment New York Volunteer Cavalry*, Poland Center, 1901.

Cooke, John Esten.   *Wearing of the Gray*, Bloomington, Indiana University Press, 1959.

Crowninshield, Benj. W. & Gleason, D.H.   *A History of the First Regiment of Massachusetts Cavalry Volunteers*, Boston, Houghton Mifflin & Co., 1891.

Davies, Henry E.   *General Sheridan*, New York, D. Appleton & Co., 1895.

Dictionary of American Biography.   New York, Charles Scribner's Sons, 1928.

Dowdey, Clifford & Manarin, L.H., Editors.   *The Wartime Papers of R.E. Lee*, Boston, Little Brown & Co., 1961.

Downey, Fairfax.   *Sound of the Guns*, New York, David McKay Co., Inc., 1955.
　　　　　　　　　　"Clash of Cavalry," David McKay Co., Inc., 1959.

133

Dyer, Frederick H. *A Compendium of the War of the Rebellion*, Des Moines, Dyer Publishing Co., 1908.

Eisenschiml, O. *The Civil War*, New York, Grosset & Dunlap, Inc., 1956.

"Encyclopedia of the Civil War," Historical Times Illustrated, 1986, Harper & Row, New York.

Foster, Alonzo. *Reminiscences and Record of the Sixth New York Veteran Volunteer Cavalry*, New Poland, 1892.

Freeman, Douglas S. *Lee's Lieutenants*, New York, Charles Scribner's Sons, 1944.
R.E. Lee, New York, Charles Scribner's Sons, 1934.

Gorgas, Josiah. *The Civil War Diary of General Josiah Gorgas*, Tuscaloosa, The University of Alabama Press, 1947.

Gracey, S.L. (Rev.). *Annals of the Sixth Pennsylvania Cavalry*, New Poland, E.H. Butler Co., 1868.

Grant, U.S. *Personal Memoirs of U.S. Grant*, New York, Charles L. Webster & Co., 1886.

Grimsley, Dan A. *Battles in Culpeper County Virginia 1861-1865 and Other Articles*, Culpeper, 1900.

Hackley, F.W. *A Report on Civil War Explosive Ordnance*, Indian Head, U.S. Navy Propellant Plant.

Harris, Malcolm H. *A History of Louisa County Virginia, 1936*.

Hackley, Woodford B. *The Little Fork Rangers*, Richmond, Dietz Printing Co., 1927.

Henry, Robert S. *The Story of the Confederacy*, Indianapolis, Bobbs-Merrill Co., 1931.

Hyndman, William. *History of a Cavalry Company*, Philadelphia, J.B. Rogers Co., 1872.

Johnson, R.U. & Buel, C.C. *Battles and Leaders of the Civil War*, New York, The Century Co., 1887.

Johnston, Angus J. II. *Disloyalty on Confederate Railroads in Virginia*, Richmond, Virginia Historical Society, October, 1955.

Kidd, J.H. *Personal Recollections of a Cavalryman with Custer's Michigan Cavalry Brigade in the Civil War*, Ionia, Sentinel Printing Co., 1908.

Lloyd, W.P. *History of the First Regiment Pennsylvania Reserve Cavalry 1861-1864*, Philadelphia, King & Baird, 1864.

Louisa County Centennial Commission. *Louisa County and the War Between the States*, Charlottesville, The Wayside Press.

McDonald, William N. *A History of the Laurel Brigade*, Baltimore, Kate S. McDonald, 1907.

Merrill, S.H. *Campaigns of the First Maine and First D.C. Cavalry*, Portland, Bailey & Noyes, 1866.

Milhollen, H.D., Johnson, J.R., and Bill, A.H. *Horsemen Blue and Gray*, New York, Oxford University Press, 1960.

Miller, Francis T. (Ed.) *The Photographic History of the Civil War*, New York, The Review of Reviews Co., 1911.

Moyer, H.P. *History of the Seventeenth Regiment Pennsylvania Volunteer Cavalry*, Lebanon, Sowers Printing Co., 1911.

Myers, Frank M. *The Comanches*, Baltimore, Kelly Piet & Co., 1871.

Naisawald, L. Van Loan. *Grape and Canister*, New York, Oxford University Press, 1960.

Neese, George H. *Three Years in the Confederate Horse Artillery*, New York, Neale Publishing Co., 1911.

Preston, N.D. *History of the Tenth Regiment of Cavalry, New York State Volunteers*, New York, D. Appleton & Co., 1892.

Pyne, Henry R. *The History of the First New Jersey Cavalry*, Trenton, J.A. Beecher, 1871.

Robert Hardy Publications, Suffolk, Virginia.

Sheridan, Philip H. *Personal Memoirs of P.H. Sheridan*, New York, Charles L. Webster & Co., 1888.

The Central Virginian, Louisa, Virginia, September 10, 1987.

Tobie, E.P. *History of the First Maine Cavalry 1861-1865*, Boston, Emery & Hughes, 1887.

Turner, Charles W. *The Virginia Central Railroad at War 1861-1865*, The Journal of Southern History, Nov. 1946.
_____ *The Education of Col. David Bullock Harris, CSA*, 1984.

Turner, George E. *Victory Rode the Rails*, New York, The Bobbs-Merrill Co., Inc., 1953.

U.S. War Department. *The War of the Rebellion: A Compilation of the Official Records of the Union and Confederate Armies*, Washington, 1880-1891, 70 vols., in 128.

Van de Water, Frederic.   *Glory Hunter. A Life of General Custer*, Indianapolis & New York, The Bobbs-Merrill Co., Inc., 1934.

Virginia Central Railroad, *Annual Reports*, Richmond, 1860-1865.

Virginia State Library, *Muster Rolls, C.S.A.*

Wallace, Lee A., Jr.   "A Guide to Virginia Military Organizations, 1861-1865," 1964.

Warner, Ezra J.   *Generals in Gray*, Baton Rouge, Louisiana State University Press, 1959.

Wells, Edward L.   *Hampton and His Cavalry in 1864*, Richmond, B.P. Johnson Pub. Co., 1899.

Wells, Edward L.   "A Sketch of the Charleston Light Dragoons," Lucas, Richardson & Co., Charleston, S.C., 1888.

Wiley, Bell I.   *The Life of Johnny Reb*, Indianapolis, The Bobbs-Merrill Co., Inc., 1943.

———— *The Life of Billy Yank*, Indianapolis, The Bobbs-Merrill Co., Inc., 1952.

Williams, Alfred B.   *Hampton and His Red Shirts*, Charleston, Walker, Evans & Cogswell Co., 1935.

Wise, J.C.   *The Long Arm of Lee*, New York, Oxford University Press, 1959.

Young, Bennett H.   *Confederate Wizards of the Saddle*, Boston, Chapple Pub. Co., Ltd., 1914.

INDEX

W

Waring, Colonel J. F., CSA, 112, 115, 127

Warley, Captain F. F., CSA, 98

Warren, Maj. Gen. G. K., USA, 47

Wells, E. L., CSA, 68

West Point, Military Museum of, 36, 37, 38

Whitcomb, H. D., 2

White House, Virginia, 25

Whitlock, J. H., 1, 2, 25

Whitner, Captain J. N., CSA, 98

Wickham, Brig. Gen. W. C., CSA, 28, 58, 93, 113

Wilds, Colonel, CSA, 98

Wilkinson, R. B., Jr., 88, 89

Wilkinson, Captain J. L., USAF, 89

Williston, Lieut. E. B., USA, 7, 28, 128

Wilson, Brig. Gen. James B., 97

Winn, Pvt. Frank, CSA, 115, 120, 122

Woolfolk's Store, 51

Wright, Colonel G. J., CSA, 6, 28, 115, 127

Y

Young's Brigade, CSA, 10, 28, 59, 71, 72, 113, 115

Young, Brig. Gen. P. M. B., CSA, 115

Z

Zimmerman, Mr. Wm., 100